Rev. Dr. Frank Alper
Moses and the Bible

Volume 1
1980

Drawing by Rev. Dr. Frank Alper

The Story of Creation

Copyright © 2024 ADAMIS - Katharina Alper

Moses and The Bible Volume 1 (of 4)
Original transcripts of the evening sessions 1980
ISBN 978-3-9524930-8-3

Edition ADAMIS
Katharina Alper
Zwydenweg 14
CH 6052 Hergiswil NW, Switzerland
Phone: +41 41 630 33 01

Email: katharina.alper@adamis.ch

Website: www.adamis.ch

Channeled through Dr. Frank Alper 1980
Editor: Katharina Alper
Layout: Katharina Alper
Cover design: Katharina Alper
Drawing of Moses: Rev. Dr. Frank Alper

Printed by: Lulu

Introduction to Volume 1

The words contained in these pages are the spiritual channelings of Frank Alper, founder of the Arizona Metaphysical Society.

These are transcripts of the weekly classes in a spiritual interpretation of the Bible and of Creation. The energies of many souls in spirit-form have contributed to the knowledge and information contained within these pages.

Dr. Frank Alper has served in the capacity of a conscious channel for many years. The transcripts of his channelings are received by many throughout the world.

The purpose of this class is not to discredit or disavow the written words of the Bible. It was merely the intention to add dimensions and encourage an expansion of interpretation of the written word. Many theories are posed to the reader without statements of finality. Individuals must create their own truth in perspective of their lives and their own realities.

We bless the energies of Moses and other spiritual Masters of sharing their knowledge and truth with us during these classes. We are grateful for the opportunity to serve our Father in this capacity to disseminate the energies of his children.

In eternal light and Love, Rev. Dr. Frank Alper

Background and Source Material

Dr. Frank Alper: A spiritual teacher who transitioned in 2007, leaving behind numerous manuscripts and recordings from over 30 years of lectures and seminars.

Channeling Sessions: The books "Moses and the Bible" and "An Evening with Christos" are based on channeling sessions conducted by Dr. Alper in Phoenix, Arizona, in the late 1970s and early 1980s.

Content and Authenticity

Transcripts: These books contain original transcripts from the channeling evenings.

Maintaining Originality: The transcripts preserve the original spoken words, even if they sometimes deviate from correct grammar. This decision ensures that the unique energy and essence of the messages are maintained.

Purpose and Usage

Energy and Wisdom: The words are not just informational but also sources of spiritual energy. Each channeled message carries the unique energy of the entity being channeled.

Reading Experience: Readers are encouraged to read the books aloud or silently, feeling the energy of the words and allowing them to resonate personally.

Interpretation: The sentences are complex and open to multiple interpretations. Readers should contemplate and find the aspects of the truth that resonate with them.

Editorial Notes

Typographical Errors: While efforts were made to correct typographical errors, some may remain due to the volume of material.

Recommendation: Readers should approach the books with an open mind, allowing the channeled words to inspire and guide them.

The original transcripts aim to provide a direct and authentic connection to Dr. Alper's spiritual teachings, offering inspiration and personal spiritual experiences.

We wish you freedom, joy and happiness in your life.

Edition Adamis, Katharina Alper

Table of Contents

Table of Contents

Chapter 12

Chapter 13

Chapter 14

Chapter 15

Chapter 16

Dr. Frank Alper: A Journey of Spiritual Discovery

Dr. Frank Alper was born on January 22, 1930, into a traditional Jewish family in Brooklyn, New York. From a young age, Frank questioned the traditions of his faith. During the ten days of repentance between Rosh Hashanah and Yom Kippur, he listened to the long list of sins he was accused of committing and couldn't understand how he could be guilty of sins he did not even comprehend. This experience sparked a lifelong quest to understand the nature of sin, God, and the Creator.

As he matured, Frank felt increasingly restless and unhappy within his tradition. His longing for deeper insight and wisdom became almost unbearable. In the 1970s, driven by his search for truth, Frank moved to Phoenix, Arizona, leaving behind his family, friends, job, and a comfortable life. With just a suitcase and a heart full of determination, he started anew, committed to finding the right answers and achieving inner peace.

During this period, Frank underwent what he referred to as his "initiations of fire," which connected him profoundly to Universal Law and solidified his integrity. His strong connection to the lost civilization of Atlantis led him to channel a body of work titled "Exploring Atlantis" in the early 1980s. This work focused on crystals and their geometric configurations and became central to his seminars.

What began with a handful of students quickly blossomed into a movement. Frank's teachings on crystal energy and his healing methods spread rapidly across North America. Affectionately known as "Crystal Daddy" by his followers, Frank's channeling sessions were renowned for their accuracy. Often, the profound truths he conveyed took time for individuals to fully integrate, revealing their significance only in retrospect.

Frank's teachings centered on the belief that all humans are children of the universe, capable of achieving anything. He emphasized that our purpose on Earth is to have spiritual experiences that expand our consciousness through the duality and freedom of life. "Your existence is mind," he often said, "and through your mind, you can create any reality you wish."

For over three decades, Frank shared his vast reservoir of spiritual knowledge and healing methods across North America, Europe, and Japan. As a universal channel, he introduced his students to a multitude of entities, masters, angels, and abstract energies. His strong connection to Moses led to the channeling of the "Spiritual Numerology of Moses," a system now known as the Soul Plan.

In the early 1980s, Frank began channeling information about the "children of the new root race," later known as Indigo or Crystal Children. He described these children with different color qualities and assigned them specific guardians, potentials, and tasks. This foresight into a new generation highlighted his role as a pioneer.

Frank's innovative spirit also led to the development of ENERGE-NETICS, a method of genetic energy reconstruction aimed at eradicating genetic conditions. Although not yet widely practiced, Frank believed this method would one day help reduce genetic illnesses, aligning with his belief that the right person would always emerge to introduce crucial advancements to humanity.

Despite the breadth of beings Frank channeled, his most significant goal was to help individuals achieve emotional freedom and balance their soul existence with earthly life. This vision guided his teachings until the very end.

In 2005, aware of his declining health, Frank referred to this period as his "final chapter." His faith in God and spirit remained unshakable, even as he sensed his days were numbered. He taught with renewed urgency, delivering his last seminar in Switzerland in October 2007. Frank Alper passed away in Switzerland on December 7, 2007, at the age of 77, leaving behind a legacy of spiritual enlightenment and healing.

Chapter 1

Moses: The six days of Creation

Bless you; this is Christos speaking.

It is indeed a great pleasure for us to feel the energies within this circle. I'm only speaking to you for a few moments, mostly in the role of introducing the energies of Moses to you, for a facet of these energies are a component of ourselves.

The project we are undertaking this night is, indeed, a momentous one, and we pray that as time progresses that your understanding of the true meaning of the words of your Father shall add dimensions to your own personal philosophies and your truth. This is the purpose for this class. It is not our intention to rewrite the Bible, but it is our intention to expose you to other interpretations in many areas to give you a greater scope of understanding and purpose of all creation. And to the extent that creation shall survive, and what man's role is within the survival. So, if you will be patient for a moment or two, we shall proceed.

Moses

I bless you; these are the energies of Moses.

I shall begin my talk to you tonight with an ancient Hebrew phrase, „Shema Yisroel, Adonay Eloheinu, Adonay Chod". It means, „Hear o Israel, the Lord is your God, the Lord is One". To interpret it further, it also means that there shall be no other Gods before Thee.

It is indeed my pleasure and honor to be allowed to discuss with you tonight, and on many future nights, the writings of the Bible and, perhaps, expand your knowledge and understanding of these treasures. From time to time, I shall inject a few principles of the

„Kabbala" that bear a direct correlation to the Bible, for there are many similarities. The main distinction being that the Kabbala in its true form and sense has never been properly written as the word itself implies, an „oral law".

It is important for all of you to understand at the outset that many of God's ancient laws were indeed „oral laws," for mankind, I total, was in those ancient days in spiritual communication with our Father. There was rarely a need for anyone to consult a seer or medium, for all had the ability to seek and hear their own truth.

The need to write, the need to create the Bible in the form of a book arose when man lost the ability and the confidence to acknowledge that he was his Father's child. He needed someone else to tell him who he was. To look, perhaps, at a particular word in order for him to be able to see, to feel that maybe this is the truth.

Many times, the master's say that every individual is a temple unto himself. If this be the true, then every individual is also a Bible unto himself, for within the temple, or the church, or the synagogue, or the shrine, rests the scrolls of the teachings of the Father.

I say to you at the outset that it is not mandatory for you to accept the words I share with you as divine truth. All that I request of you is to hear my words, ponder them, disagree with them, and question until the statement has been resolved in your minds. There shall be times when I will pose trick questions to you to see if you are keeping yourself alert and not blindly heeding and accepting my words.

For those of you who need an answer to a specific question, I shall answer it for you now. The soul of Moses does indeed carry a great portion of energies of the Christ-Spirit, much as the Master Jesus did along with many others who walked to face of this planet in service for our Father.

Let us begin at the beginning. Within the bindings of every Bible that has ever been complied, the opening words are as follows: God created the heavens and the Earth in six days, and when the sixth day was done, and he found his work completed, he chose the seventh day as a day of rest, a day for what we now call the Sabbath. Is the Sabbath on Saturday, on Sunday, on Friday? Who has determined what day of the current week was the first day? There were no clocks or English calendars to let one know when a twenty-four-hour cycle had ended.

What then is a day? If we are to look at the Bible literally, and if we are still young children, we must relate to the word „day" as we know a day to be. Under those circumstances, indeed, there has been a miracle of miracles, for it is almost beyond the comprehension of the human mind to create all of this: the water, the earth, the planets, the heavens, the subterranean caverns etc., in a span of six times twenty-four. Isn't it interesting, six times twenty-four? It totals one hundred forty-four, or twelve or twelve.

Therefore, this brings us to a realization that perhaps we are dealing with something other than system of time as we know it. Perhaps we are dealing with a system of vibrations. Perhaps we are dealing with a system of facets of energy, for as we know the complete division of energy force is at optimum within the division of twelve.

In essence, the creation of this planet, the evolution of this vibrations to enable it to contain life and vegetation involved a span of millions upon millions upon millions of years. You are Children of Light. Dare you think that this planet Earth was the first planet to be created and sustain life within the confines of this Universe?

This is the indication that is derived from reading that portion of the Bible, and yet, we know this is not so.

The strata of life incarnated on and within this planet evolved as the vibrations of the planet itself evolved over the course of time. Millions of years ago there were forms of animal and vegetable life that suffered extinction due to the eventual incompatibility of their vibrations with the changing planet. There were many species of life destroyed during Earth changes and the ice ages, but as a rule, their destruction resulted from incompatibility of vibration.

If we are to listen to the seers and sages who relate stories of alien beings who came to incarnate on this planet from other worlds, and tell us that they are here because their own planet is no longer capable of sustaining their existence, then why should our energy evolution on this planet be different?

There is a story at the beginning of Genesis relating to two beautiful souls, Adam, and Eve. The third part of the triangle is the Garden of Eden. Once again, we have a trinity: male, female, and motherlove. I doubt that there is one amongst you who in your early years of religious studies ever thought that the Garden of Eden was anything else but a small plot of ground containing lush, beautiful forests, trees, fruit and honey, a paradise. Yet, if we look at the symbolic meaning behind these words, and we take the trinity of Adam and Eve and the Garden of Eden and place it inside the circle of our Father's Light, we are then thinking of the planet as a whole. We are thinking of a planet created to house perfection, to be a total expression of love.

Did Eve sin, or was she guilty of exercising her free will? How do you wish to look at it? Does it become „sin" because one is caught in an act, and not „sin" if another is not caught with the same stimulus to take the action?

Let us use the word „strayed" rather than „sinned". Let us try these words on for size: perhaps the story of Adam and Eve does not relate to only two people. Perhaps it pertains to a race of people. Perhaps the „apple" represents human temptation expressed in any one of many forms. Perhaps the snake symbolizes the utilization of free will, the first involvement in choice. Perhaps it is the pattern of evolution for mankind to afford him opportunities to express himself in a variety of ways.

The Garden of Eden is as lush and as fertile and pure as your mind allows it to be. For some, it is a slithering snake in a swamp. For others, it is row upon row of roses and perfumed flowers.

We, mankind, you and I, are born of a vibration. It is as a tuning fork, for it has resonance, intensity, and frequency. The more we heed our music, the more we are in God's symphony.

We are going to end our discussion at this point. During the rest of the class let us discuss that I have posed to you this evening.

Bless you.

Chapter 2

Moses: The Cleansing of Earth

Bless you: these are the energies of Moses.

Once again it is my pleasure to share with you again this night. It is often said that history repeats itself, and perhaps the story that we shall discuss this night has yet to repeat itself and let us hope and pray that it shall not come to pass. When the Children of God, the descendants of symbolic Adam and Eve populated the Earth in multitudes as the sands of the desert, they erred in their ways and strayed in their path. The Bible says that God came to one called Noah whom he found in his favor and told him to prepare a mighty ship. It would house a representation of all species of life existing on this planet. He felt that he was ashamed for the creation of man, for they were not worthy to walk in his Light. He wished to cleanse the planet.

Let us look at this story up to this point from a different perspective. Within our spiritual philosophy and beliefs, we understand that even God does not sit in judgement. His function is love. If this be the case, who then made the decision? Was it perhaps man himself? Was it perhaps masses of negative energy that man projected that instigated the cleansing of the planet? Did man serve as his own judge? There was a ship hundreds of feet long and hundreds of feet wide, a ship in a time when, supposedly, tools such as we know them today were non-existent. Water proofing materials were nowhere to be found, and yet they said the ship was constructed of such enormous strength that it could house and contain the weight of species of every living creature.

Ezekiel talks in the Bible of a descending Light, of a vehicle with wheels within wheels. He talks of ships from space that landed, of men that walked the face of the Earth. So, let me pose to you a statement neither affirming nor denying. Is it possible that the vehicle that Noah supposedly constructed was, in fact, a ship from your Space Brothers sent on a mission to save the human race?

A scribe who writes, who fills the pages of a book reads ancient parchments that talk of a ship. Where would he in his wildest dreams imagine it would be anything other than a crudely constructed ark from lumber and timbers. Yet, the possibility exists. The correlation between the then and the now is strong. At this very moment, your Space Brothers are circling this planet hoping they shall not be needed in a similar situation, for if this planet is to be destroyed it is mankind who shall do it and no other.

The Bible talks of the ages of man during that era in figures of five, six, seven, eight and nine hundred years life spans. Yet, mankind today considers himself to be blessed upon reaching one hundred years of age. It is considered an oddity. Is it, in truth, a lie? Did man, in reality, live hundreds and hundreds of our years? The answer is yes, of course. In the sinning, the leaving of the Path, to sustain life no longer functioned properly. Life is truly an alchemic reaction.

So, we find that when the waters receded, and the purification and the cleansing of this planet was complete, and the symbolic Dove that Noah sent out to seek and find dry land did not return indicating the end of the deluge, the span of man's life has already been readjusted to approximately one hundred and seventy-five years, with some exceptions.

Can you imagine what it would be like to return to a land laid waste, to know that so many have perished, that you are to start anew? And so, the seeds of Noah were multiplied, and his children and his children's children once again multiplied as grains of sand on the desert. From these seeds came two, one known as Abram, one known as Sarai, familiar to you as Abraham and Sarah. But these were not the names of their birth. For numerological reasons, their names were changed to alter their vibrations and allow Sarai to conceive.

In all areas of the history of the world, the evolutions of civilizations, we find the action and reaction, the active and the passive, or the positive and the negative. So, we have the relationship between Abraham and Lot: one man of love, one man of greed, one of brotherhood, and one of hate.

When the Earth was cleansed, and the waters rose over the highest mountains on the planet purifying every square inch of ground, our Father made a decision to use this planet as a testing ground. I say to you that prior to that time it was intended to be a Garden of Eden. But the misuse and the abuse caused the destruction, and so within the time span it took for the waters to rise not only from rain but also from earthquakes and tidal waves, until that time when the waters totally receded covered a span of twelve hundreds of your years. During that time additional vibrations were placed within the atmosphere surrounding this planet to expose mankind to new forms of vibrations and experiences. Beginning at that time we saw the initiation of the use of this planet as a means for justifying and assimilating karmic lessons.

No longer was mankind entitled to his „Garden of Eden". Henceforth, he must strive and work to earn way and his path back to his Father. Before this time that balance between the positive and the negative truly did not exist. After the flood, for every civilization that walked in the Light there was one that walked in darkness. For every king that ruled with love, there was one that ruled with hate.

For every child that loved his brother there was one that slew his brother and pillaged and looted.

When God came to Abraham, then called Abraham, he was almost seventy-five of your years. He spoke to him, and he blessed him, and he told him to take himself and his possessions and go to the land of Cannan, a dry, arid, baked desert. Why did he do this? It was to create the balance, and the desert flourished. The symbolism behind Abram has been repeated hundreds of times throughout history, and, in truth, is repeated with each of you every day of your lives every time you are called upon to do service for your Father, to take an action, to take an action without questioning, to have faith for all, for faith is all that you have.

The child that Sarai bore when becoming Sarah, was it truly a child as we know it, or was it a much broader manifestation? Was it a dimension added to a whole new set of vibrations, vibrations of rebirth by spirit? Was that perhaps the first immaculate conception? By our standards, the woman was far beyond the years of childbearing.

What role have other worlds; other civilizations played in the growth of this Planet? How much assistance has mankind received to help him find his path and survive, or did he do it all by himself? Perhaps Noah truly did not build an ark of wood, for all is possible. The truth us within your mind. The lies are within your emotions.

These are the words that I share with you this night. I have said much, and yet, perhaps I have said nothing. So, in a few moments let us discuss what you have heard. Let us stimulate your minds, and perhaps allow all to reach a conclusion, for this indeed, is my true purpose for being here with you, to raise your doubts, to urge you to seek your truth.

You are sitting here in your mastery. Rise above the material vibrations and seek the causes from your spiritual essence. Accept your obligations of divine truth and bring it to your consciousness so that you may walk in your light.

Bless you.

Chapter 3

The Father: Universal Law

Bless you, I speak to you tonight with the energies of your Father, for the context of the message this night is if such importance that He has desired to impart these words to you Himself.

We talk to you tonight of covenant, of law, for you must understand that law, as it was passed to the Children so many thousands of years ago has, indeed, changed and grown and developed. As the soul grows and develops the laws must also expand and grow to accommodate the new knowledge and the development that the individual soul has achieved. Perhaps it is better said that the laws themselves, as they are handed and given to you are not complete. You receive at a stage in your development a partial law. As you grow, more and more of the scope of total overall law itself is revealed to you to better facilitate you understanding and comprehension of the laws. So, many of the ancient laws do not apply verbatim at this particular time.

Whenever a child has appeared and assumes a physical incarnation to serve a special role for Me, when he has reached maturity within the incarnation and is ready to assume his service contract, a covenant is established between Us.

A covenant was established between Noah and Myself, for he was required to stand alone, to take the ridicule of his fellow man, to outward appearance to dream, to dream the impossible, and yet, have the faith. Without the bond, vibration the seal of energies, without the oneness of the vibration his total divine dedication would have been impossible. Once it was established, once the devotion to purpose unwavering and unchangeable.

15

Let us move ahead in history to the story of Abraham and Isaac. It was necessary several times during the life of Abraham to make separate covenants for each phase of his growth and each phase of his responsibility. New strength and dedication were required to enable him to overcome the obstacles he faced. What man in his right mind who had waited a hundred years for a son would, upon the word of an impression on his mind, take a knife and prepare to slay his son for his Father? I dare say none of you know such a man.

In essence, is there any difference between the covenant of Abraham and Isaac then when you are asked by your masters to release yourself to your Father's energies. When you are asked to place your entire being and welfare in the hands of your Father, to walk His path and allow Him to guide you, to steer your life. The results are the same. A release is effected, a total release. No longer are you totally only responsible to yourself, for within the covenant you and your Father are One. This responsibility is now a joint one for every action you undertake during the course of your lives.

Mankind refers to this as relinquishing his free will. Is it truly a relinquishing, or is it a blending of purpose and will with that of your Father to acknowledge the Oneness? The key to the apprehension involved in making this covenant is self-worth, faith in your ability to be worthy of the oneness. Once this has been conquered the actual mechanics of making and accepting the covenant becomes fairly simple. It becomes the normal course of action for you.

A man named Abraham was asked by God to leave, to leave his lands, and live in a dry, arid desert, to begin anew, to have the faith that he would have a child, a son, where no man had had a son before. Would it have been possible to have such absolute faith in the impossible, to say yes at all levels of consciousness without knowing in the depths of the heart that this Oneness existed with God? This then was the key at that time and is the key at this present day. The mighty deeds and sacrifices that have been made by the ancient masters were only able to be carried out to completion because of the Oneness with the Father.

I am going to discuss with you at this time a few areas of „The Law". In the future, from time to time, we shall bring you more and more of spiritual law as it pertains and relates at that time.

We talk about the „Law of private Domain". Each man is entitled to own and amass property whether it be a single plot of land, a large area, a state, a country, an island, as long as he has procured it by honorable methods and hard work. No one is required to be denied assets. No one is required to destitute, to be suffering from a lack in order to prove one's devotion to the Father. All are entitled to acquire possessions. All are allowed and encouraged to protect their possessions and their property in honor, and with honorable means.

If, within the „Law of Private Domain", one abuses the flow of substance that has come to him, one shall surely lose it. All must understand and know that all substance is in a constant state of flow, and never rests. It is acquired to be used fruitfully and productively. If once acquired it is allowed to lay fallow, it soon dissipates.

„Thou shall not covet they neighbor's wife". In ancient biblical days this law was interpreted to an extreme literal degree. One would not approach a friend's wife and ask her to lunch, so to speak. If chance meeting accrued between the two, each would go their separate ways. Communication and association were frowned upon except in the presence of the spouses.

Today we understand far more. Today mankind is aware of the sensing vibrations, of the sending of a different aspect of his life.

He is encouraged to „love they neighbor's wife." I speak of love within this area in terms of spiritual vibrations, of walking with one's heart open that other may feel and share your love, to una-shamedly extend and offer it to all, not to walk your arms crossing your chest, hiding yourself from fellow man, containing what you have to offer inside of yourself instead of sharing freely with your brothers and sisters. The word, „covet", means desire, desire in a carnal sense. You who sit here are not carnal beings. You are awak-ened Children of love. You are aware of your identities. You no longer have the capacity to be carnal within your emotions, for if you were to attempt to do so, it would destroy you.

You are expressions of your vibrations. You are expressions of your love. Not one of you should carry shame for this.

„Thou shalt not steal". During the time of Moses, this law was in-terpreted to mean, thou shalt not take what visibly and physically is not yours. This aspect of this law is still in force. However, the scope of the law has increased a hundred-fold. Today we are aware of those who would take of your vibrations, who would at-tempt to transmute your love into negativity, who would drain you of your strength, who would tempt you and try to sway you from your path. A vibration is sacred unto one who has nourished it. One who „steals" vibrations draws a most sever lesson.

At this point I wish to turn this discussion to another area, and yet an area related to this law. We are going to touch quite lightly on this area now, and discuss it in depth several weeks from now, when we have reached the area in the Scriptures relating to this topic. It is felt that an introduction, a posing to your minds is nec-essary, so we shall begin.

As you know, the atmosphere surrounding this planet is filled with your space brothers and sisters. They are here to protect and service you if the time for their help arises. There are also those in ships around this planet from other planets who seek to harm and destroy. This is not conjecture. I say this to you in My truth.

Within the center of the core of this planet are worlds inhabited by living physical beings. Under the seas of this planet are extremely highly evolved souls and have been in place since the beginning. It is they and their energies and abilities that are in communication and direct the actions of many of the space fleets around this planet. They guide and correlate their functions. They also serve to dissuade and turn actions against this planet. Think about it. As above, so below: the balance from the inside, as well as from the outside.

When we reach the area of the Bible relating to these subterranean worlds, we shall bring you their vibrations to allow you to sense them, to speak to them, to experience their communications and their worlds. Their vibrations are unlike any you have experienced before due to their texture and nature. Yet you shall find them positive and in love.

Creation, in all its simplicity, is complex. The balance of a planet is within itself as complex as the balance of this Universe. Throughout history, those in the core of the planet have had as their responsibility the effecting of many changes within the surface of this planet. They work and act according to directions from the Great Council whose responsibility it is for the continuation an evolution of this planet.

The great vortexes of energy that emanate from the ground to the surface of this planet are all beams of communications: energy, light, emanating from the core. These vortexes are vibrations, transmuting negativity that spread throughout this planet. They also serve as beacons for communication into space, and many other functions relating to your space brothers and sisters. They are also used to effect the alignment of the planet, the orbiting axis of this planet, and many other functions.

And so, what appears to the naked eye to be a simple group of men, a man willing to sacrifice his only son for his Father, is, in fact, a highly complex chain of vibrations, one interacting upon the other.

I have said to you this night what I have said to you so that you would understand that all rules progress according to Divine Law, that at all times, at any given moment, what must be, shall be. When, in an isolated instance, an action is taken against the vibrations of your Father, it creates a cause, and the cause creates an effect, and the effect can be multiplied in magnitude and intensity. An assassination can lead to a war. A careless match can create a fire. But, in the end all shall be, for in truth, I AM.

I Bless you, My Children.

Chapter 4

Moses: Universal Law.

These are the energies of Moses, and we Bless you.

Before we begin our discussion tonight of Jacob and his sons, we wish to discuss one more of God's Laws with you, the law relating to "Thou shalt not steal".

Perhaps the law in today's context should be reworded to state, "Thou shalt obey the Laws of Substance and Prosperity," for if all practiced the Laws of Substance and Prosperity the word, "steal", would not apply in your language, or in any language. All would understand that substance is in a constant state of flow, that all one's needs are available to be drawn from the Universal Substance as the need is created and expressed. The need to steal arises when one tries to retain, to hold onto substance, to stop the flow, to amass the substance, considering it his or hers. This creates greed, the desire to hoard leading to the urges to steal. If man will accept the fact that he is merely a channel for substance to flow to and then through, he will find peace, for his needs shall be fulfilled.

To steal is to interrupt the flow of Universal Substance. For this one most assuredly draws karma. Know that the karma is not for the act of stealing, it is for the act of interrupting the flow of substance.

Jacob and His Sons

Now let us proceed to the topic for tonight's discussion. There was Abraham, Issac and then Jacob, when Jacob was on in years, he had given seed to twelve sons, two by Rachael and the balance by Leah and the two maidservants. This caused a diversity of blood lines, a diversity of genes, and a diversity of souls incarnating within these twelve sons. Of the twelve, the two most famous in history are Joseph and Benjamin, and for a while we shall talk of Joseph, he of the coat of many colors. He is the son upon whom the Father bestowed through God's Hand all the energies of wisdom and love expressed through Light and Color. For indeed, the coat of many colors was a very powerful symbol for Joseph.

Joseph was an emissary sent by our Father to begin a long chain of actions and reactions involving the Hebrews and the Egyptians. Joseph was at all times in communication with his Father at the conscious level. He spoke his Father's Word in all situations where a question was posed to him. Consequently, he was placed in a position of great authority and power within Egypt. In effect, he was single-handedly responsible for the survival of the Egyptian civilization spanning the time of seven years of feast and seven years of famine.

Why were there seven years of feast and seven years of famine? Were these periods truly seven of our years? Were they, perhaps, shorter, or longer? What was their function? Truly, God would not impose a situation or ordeal of this nature upon not only the Egyptian nation, but upon surrounding nations without a Divine Purpose at hand. Let us suppose the purpose was to assimilate the Hebrews and the Egyptians, to teach them to live in unity and as one, to interchange and interrelate their cultures, for all to grow united with God. For is it not true that during the years of the famine Joseph was allowed to bring Jacob and his brothers and the balance of their tribes to settle in Goshen to live and assimilate? Isn't it strange that before this occurred God came to Jacob and changed his name to Israel to give him the vibrations of a nation. It was to plant the vibration within his tribe of nationality rather than that of nomad and wanderer.

Let us take ourselves back in time for a few moments. Let us return to Atlantis near the end, to the time when destruction was imminent, when many of the Elders of Atlantis were removed or passed to avoid unnecessary suffering, and then were asked by their Father to incarnate on the surface of the Earth to continue their work and growth, to unite the peoples on Earth under God's Laws.

Jacob's name in Atlantis was spelled Urian. Joseph's name in Atlantis was spelled Boral. Do we not have an analogy here? Do we not have Jacob and his twelve sons, as we had Jesus and his twelve disciples? Is it not as we have Spirit Core and its twelve divisions?

All of the sons of Jacob were incarnated from the souls of the Ancients of Atlantis carefully selected and chosen to bring within each facet of the twelve different expressions. This was done so that their children might grow and learn from all expressions. Each of Jacob's sons bore many sons who bore many sons, and they multiplied, and theirs multiplied. The first sons of the sons were also the Elders from Atlantis, and from the sons of the sons originated the Twelve Tribes of Israel. They were composed of the Ancients of Atlantis.

The opportunity existed to create a "Garden of Eden," to live in harmony and peace and unity. But the snake once again coiled, and fear rose in the hearts of many Egyptians in the Pharaoh's court. The Law of Prosperity was pushed aside, and greed and stealing took precedence over love. The fear grew, and the Pharaoh ordered the midwives to slay the children, born male, of the Hebrew wives. When this failed, he ordered the sons to be thrown into the rivers. Is this not greed? Is this not stealing? And so, instead of brothers a nation became enslaved.

One young mother, for fear of her son's life, took him and put him afloat in the river in a basket of rushes in hopes that someone would find him and rear him and love him. Thus began the story of my life, my life as Moses.

The incarnation as Moses was not an easy one for me to assume. I had finished long tenure ruling in Atlantis and wished to rest. However, service for our Father is eternal, and so my story began. I will not go into great detail during the younger years of my life, but I will bring you to the point when under our Father's Direction, I asked the Pharaoh to release our people, to allow us to leave so that we might pursue our lives in peace and harmony. This request was denied; once again to steal, to steal our right to our lives.

The Bible talks of plagues, and the last one retribution - the slaying of the first-born Egyptian sons. There is a story, a dissertation written by a man who states that at the time of the occurring of the plagues, the vibrations and magnetic fields of the planet Earth were drastically affected by the close passing of a comet of enormous dimensions, that it to a degree effected a slight shift in the Earth's axis, that to a degree slightly effected the orbit of this planet, and perhaps caused what is referred to in the written word as the plagues.

This is not to imply that the plagues were an accident, for God's Hand works in many strange ways. The result is the same. Would you believe me if I told you that I was guided across the desert by communication with your space brothers? Would you believe me if I stated to you, in truth, that an earthquake caused the Red Sea to part? Or better shall I say, effected the sea to part, for the cause, of course, was our Father.

I must say to you in all truth there were many times during my life, and more so during our journey through the desert, when my devotion to God was sorely tested, more than it is possible to imagine. Many times, I came close to turning from my path. I did not know why, why I was chosen to suffer so, why I was chosen for such responsibility. For there were indeed many times during the journey when I was denied spiritual guidance to test my blind faith in our Father, to feel deserted and yet know that I was not deserted. I did not understand. It was not part of my conscious thoughts that perhaps I was, even at that time, being prepared for future missions for God, for future incarnations for our Father.

For you see, I have also been Augustus of Rome; David of Israel; Napoleon, and several others. Even during the time when so many untold thousands of lives depended upon my guidance, my faith, I was being prepared for other things. I mention this to you not for my edification. I mention this to you for your own lives' when you question, at times, "why me, why do I need to go through this?"

Each soul has its Divine Plan. For me the lesson at that time was indeed one of Divine faith and acceptance of God's Will at all levels. Without it surely our mission, our freedom would have been denied. In time many of those of the original Twelve Tribes of Israel, and they are called Twelve Tribes of Israel, for they are the sons of Jacob who became Israel, made pilgrimages to many other areas of the world. They were to bring God's Word to other civilizations existing throughout the four corners of the globe. History does not record the total lineage of the twelve tribes. Some may say that they dissipated and faded into obscurity. This is not true. Many of them were totally assimilated into other cultures quite alien to their own, but this too was their mission.

It is for this reason that many ancient writings in different cultures throughout the world record events happening simultaneously in different areas of the planet. The vibrations, the teachings, the laws were of the same texture and quality.

Let us all ponder and concern ourselves with the words I have shared with you this night. There are many things I have said to you in conjecture to perhaps stimulate your minds. Yet, all I have said to you is truth. These are the words I bring you this night.

I Bless you.

Chapter 5

Moses: His Story and the Plagues

Bless you. These are the energies of Moses speaking.

It is our pleasure once again to share vibrations and truth with you. We speak to you this evening of attitudes, for attitudes played a large role in the course of history, in the course of events of the time the Hebrew people were enslaved by the Pharaohs.

When our Father first came to me and revealed Himself to me by the burning bush that would not burn, and told me of His Plans for me, when He told me that I, and I alone was to lead the people, the Hebrew people out of bondage and servitude, I was terribly frightened and insecure. I felt totally unworthy of such a monumental task. I did not consider myself fluent of tongue, nor having strength of words to carry out such a project.

At first, I rebelled and asked our Father to find someone else. The feeling was no different than what many of you feel when something spiritual occurs for you and you ask, "why me, why not someone else?" The answer is, of course, because you are you and not someone else. I pleaded with the Lord, I pleaded with Him to allow my brother, my brother Aaron to be my spokesman, he of the fluent tongue. I wished to take him with me and be my strength. Our Father became angry at my lack of faith, at my attitude.

I had not accepted the fact that He would be with me to guide me and to steer my direction. My mind was weak, and so our Father agreed to allow Aaron to serve as my spokesman. Aaron was strong. When our Father spoke to him and told him of the plans, he agreed wholeheartedly to serve in any capacity for our Father. He believed in the Lord and in himself.

I was given some tools by our Father, tools to show the Pharaoh who I was and Who I represented. It did not seem possible to me that I could walk up to the Pharaoh and announce, "you must let the Hebrews go, our Lord has said to let them go." I felt that he would laugh at me and say, who am I? The Lord told me to find a staff and to throw the staff on the ground. I did, and it became a snake. When I grabbed the snake at the tail, it once again became a staff.

This was to be the sign, the sign that I was indeed a messenger of our Father. Many people believed that when Aaron and I first approached the Pharaoh to ask him to allow the Hebrew people to leave that I was still a young man. In truth, my age had already reached eighty years. When we approached the court of the Pharaoh, he spoke for me. I had him throw the staff on the ground, and it became a snake. The Pharaoh called in his wise men, his seers, his men of magic. With their arts they too turned a staff into a snake. I said to myself, why has the Lord permitted this? If I am to impress upon the Pharaoh that I am the Lord's Emissary, why has He negated my gift? I was deeply puzzled. The Pharaoh told me to leave his presence, that he would not allow the Hebrews to leave Egypt.

An anger rose and rose greatly. He ordered those in charge of the Hebrew slaves not to supply them with straw for the bricks that the Hebrews were making. To force the Hebrews to find their own straw without decreasing their day's production of bricks, an impossible task. The Hebrews became angry and turned against me. They cried, "look what you have done. You and the Lord have doomed us, for we cannot do our work and we shall surely die."

Why did our Father do this? What was His Reason for allowing this to take place? For, if I was to free the Hebrew people, why had I only increased their suffering? It came to my mind that perhaps their faith in God was shallow enough that all that was necessary was one setback to turn them against their Father. Perhaps it had been a test of their devotion and faith in God even though it caused them great personal suffering. I was deeply troubled and riddled with guilt. I beseeched the Lord for guidance, for an explanation. He said to me, "Take the staff I have given you, go back to the Pharoah, tell him to let your people go, or you shall turn all the water in Egypt into blood."

I could not do this, and once again I took Aaron with me to speak on my behalf. We repeated the Lord's Words to the Pharaoh, and he laughed. I took the staff and touched the river with it, and moved the staff in four directions, and all the rivers turned to blood. Even the water in the jars in the homes turned to blood. The Pharaoh was disturbed and once again called upon his magicians, and once again they were also able to turn water into blood. I was sent away in anger once again.

What has my Father done? How am I to win? How am I to succeed? And I questioned our Father. I went to pray, to ask once again for Divine guidance. I said to our Father, "You have promised Your children a land of milk and honey, and yet with each attempt at freedom the situation grows more severe." Our Father said to me, "Go back to the Pharaoh. Tell him to allow you to take the Hebrew people out of Egypt. If he does not, the country shall be overrun with frogs that shall spring out of the bloody waters and shall be everywhere." Aaron and I returned once again to the Pharoah and related the Lord's Message to him. He denied our request once again.

I raised the staff and the frogs abounded. Once again, the Pharaoh's magicians were able to duplicate my feat, and I was dismissed.

Attitude. Let us consider the following possibility: Perhaps if I had entered the 'Pharaoh's presence, firm of convictions, positive in attitude, believing totally in my Father's words, maybe the Pharaoh's magicians might not have been able to duplicate the miracles I created through God. Was it then a return of energies from an attitude of lack of confidence? Was I that unsure of our Father's ability that I allowed the energies for that type of a reaction to manifest itself? Was it then my fault?

Many of God's children are asked to do seemingly impossible things, to walk seemingly impossibly roads in absolute faith that they are being properly directed by their Father. This is perhaps the most difficult aspect of your lives, for in itself it requires an absolute, total release to your Father.

The plagues continued. With each ensuing plague the Hebrews suffered more and more and more. Their bitterness, their anger against me and against our Father grew in intensity. The more their anger grew, the more severe was the next plague. Our Father had promised Abraham and Issac and Jacob to watch over and protect the Hebrew children. However, the attitude created the negative energies that brought down their miseries upon themselves and multiplied them. I feared for my life from my own people, for there were those who wished to stone me to death for what I had done to their lives, and for the restrictions that had been placed on them due to my actions. In truth, all that was necessary was for them to have faith that I was walking and being guided by God's Hand.

Throughout history man has suffered the symbolic anger of God. I say symbolic, for it is of man's own creation because of his attitude, for he expects something for nothing. This brings us to a point where I must relate to you one of our Father's Laws.

The law is stated as follows: "Once man has acknowledged the existence of God, he can no longer at any time ever deny this existence." If this occurs, then that man shall draw unto himself the most severest of lessons. We see this lesson, this law, being violated time and time again. We see people entering a house of worship on a Holy Day to ask for forgiveness for their sins. Once having paid and said their penance, they heave a deep sigh and return to their sordid ways for another year. What have they accomplished? Have they absolved themselves? Quite the contrary, for in asking for absolution they have admitted to themselves and to God the errors they have consciously committed during the course of their lives. For that, they have brought upon themselves a lesson, a lesson of magnitude as they have left the place of worship to repeat the action once again.

This story is not new; it is as old as the annals of time. We cannot wash away our actions. We cannot wish away our actions. When we call upon God to help us, He is there. Once he is there, He is always there and can never again be denied. Throughout the early history of the Hebrews this has been the single greatest cause of their suffering. Too many times they turned from their Father. I do not say to you that it is easy for a man to accept the words of one that comes and says to them, "I am here as an emissary of your Father. He has spoken to me, and I bring His Words to you in truth." One cannot expect mankind to accept such a statement openly, and yet it must be done. For if one walks with God, one knows his truth when he hears it. One feels the truth within the vibrations of the speaker. One must assume the attitude of faith. Is mankind's lot any different today than it was when the Hebrews were enslaved by the Pharaoh and forced to make bricks out of clay and straw? Has not mankind enslaved itself once again, turned itself from its Father, imposed upon itself great restrictions of behavior and attitude? Is not mankind once again being exposed to plagues? It is not the form of the plague that matters, it is the result. There is a plague of pollution. There is a plague of energy. There is a plague of political unrest. Are they any different? The end result is the same: fear, attitude.

What would happen to the energy situation if every man, woman and child ceased to concern themselves about it, accepted the situation exactly as it is in peace, without fear, without panic. The crisis would disappear, for what is, is. With faith one survives.

When I was three months old the woman who bore me had enough faith in God to leave my future in His Hands, that if it be His Will, I would survive. Her faith and her action ensured my survival. Indeed, if she had been riddled with fear and anxiety and doubt, perhaps someone else would be speaking to you this night.

In our travels through the Bible, we shall come across situations again and again that have resulted in catastrophe due to a reaction from attitudes. Mankind's existence is based on faith, on faith in God, and faith in self in relation to God. The Oneness between the two.

These are the words that we share with you this night. Look into your minds, search your souls. Examine your attitudes, for they have a strong bearing upon your growth and upon your achieving the total stability within yourself.

We Bless you for sharing with us this night.

Chapter 6

Christos: Spiritual Law

Bless You. This is Christos speaking.

We speak to you this night with the energies of your Father, for due to the nature of the topic for tonight's discussion, it is fitting that He relate the words to you Himself, for they are His Words.

We are going to discuss spiritual law with you this evening. The words inscribed on the tablets known as the Ten Commandments are laws relating to the behavior of man to his brother, and to man within the structure of the society in which he lives. Truly, some of the laws as written at that time cannot be directly applied at this time, for as societies grow and expand, laws also must grow and expand.

The spiritual law is indeed contained within the unwritten doctrine knows as the Kabbala or Kabbalah. It was impossible to have true spiritual law inscribed for posterity, for at any given moment mankind was not totally prepared to observe the law, to totally accept the law. Each individual must grow into the awareness and acceptance of spiritual law individually. Yet, each is eternally subject to the law. The law contains the basic foundation and energies under which man commences and endures his patterns of lessons and growth. It is the basic guideline under which all souls develop and evolve. So, We shall begin at the beginning.

"Thou shalt not deny the existence of God, for He is your only Reality." I say to you that I AM, and all else is lies, for all else is a variable that changes at all times. Only I AM is a constant. Therefore, when you take it upon yourselves to deny My Existence, your total existence becomes a lie. If an individual, during the course of an incarnation, consciously accepts My Presence within his being and his life, once accepted, it cannot be denied. The taking of this type of action truly draws the most severe lesson to the individual, for it is a total judgment of one's truth, of one's only reality. For this the individual within a future incarnation shall have an intense desire to find the God within and shall have a difficult time in doing so. He shall be denied this opportunity until it is recognized that the desire is totally his truth.

"For every cause there is an effect." Who has the capability of creating causes? Is this opportunity available to all at any given moment? Most assuredly not. In order to create causes, one must be as one with the I AM within themselves. One must walk in their truth and live it, for the ability to create causes carries with it a weighty responsibility. With each cause created many, many are affected. I am the Lord your God, and you are to say, "I am You, and You are I, and I have totally accepted Your Love and Truth within my vibrations. Therefore, I have achieved eternal peace and understanding. All my needs shall be fulfilled, for I am as One with my Father and need have no concerns. This total union has relieved me of all concerns, and when it is proper to create a cause, it shall be done."

We talk about the "Law of Acceptance". The Law of Acceptance can also be called the Law of Understanding. It is man's responsibility to accept the Word of his Father and understand it. This cannot be easily achieved, for during early stages of growth mankind finds itself saddled to ask why, to have needs for explanations. Only upon unification when one has accepted their Oneness can one also accept the Word for just being the Word.

We talk of the "Law of Karma". We talk of opportunities available to work out lessons incurred between two souls. The law is firm. Many times, man has said, "I am in misery in my life for a lesson I have incurred with one who is still in spirit form." This is invalid. Vibrations incurred in the physical must be worked out in the physical. Spirit is in a total vibration of love. A lesson acquired by a soul does not necessarily have to be worked out with the same soul with whom it was incurred. When this is done, it usually is done on a voluntary basis to assist the soul who has incurred the lesson.

We talk of the Law, "Thou shalt not judge." Who plays the role of judge? Do not ask Me if I sit in judgment, for I have created children of Love who need no judgment. Within the structure of the law there is a section relating to total judgment of self. This assumes many forms: insanity, spiritual possession, total failure to accept one's role within society, becoming dependent upon the state for sustenance and survival, and the most severe form of self-judgment known as suicide. What occurs when a soul makes transition and becomes aware of the total judgment it has placed upon itself during the course of an incarnation? It understands what it has done. It elects to work out these vibrations as rapidly as possible, for this type of lesson cannot be carried forth for great periods of time.

I wish to relate a story to you pertaining to judgment. Let us return to Egypt during the time of the Ten Plagues where in the end it was deemed that the first-born son of every Egyptian family was to die. Indeed, it came to pass, and the Hebrews were released from bondage. Was this indeed a judgment on My part, or was there a balance effected? If so, what was the balance? When the laws were handed to Moses, he was informed that the first-born son of every Hebrew family from that moment, for all eternity, belonged to God, that the parents of that child have to relinquish it to God, not in a physical death, but in a spiritual oneness.

Then, with the proper attitude, with the proper condition, they were allowed to "borrow" the child back from God to bear it and raise it in love, and so the balance was achieved.

To this day you shall find, My Children, that within a family the first-born son is a spiritual son, for he has become one with his Father.

We talk of the law pertaining to soul evolution. The law states that when a soul has evolved to a pre-determined level it has earned the right to end its series of karmic physical incarnations and assimilate within the vibrations of the Spirit Core. At that point it is the soul's choice to either immediately begin new levels of evolution, or to voluntarily remain within the present vibrations to do service in assisting other souls who have not yet completed their patterns. A soul may not avoid its obligations of growth. A soul may not defer serious infractions that have incurred lessons for itself. A soul may not interfere with the normal course of vibrations within a civilization on any occupied planet. A soul, whether in spirit or physical form, may not cross over and interfere in other spheres of vibrations without requesting permission to do so.

We talk of the "Law of Spiritual Fidelity". Who does it pertain to? Does it pertain to souls that have established a union of vibrations for themselves, or does it pertain only to the soul and his Father? For as it was written on the tablets given to Moses, "Thou shalt have no other Gods before Me." We talk of the "Law of Fertility". Is it man's or woman's right to alter themselves so that they may not bear children? Is it not feasible within your minds that if it is within the destiny of their lives to have a child that they shall have a child, as has occurred so many times throughout history?

The words I have spoken to you to this point have been passed down from initiate to initiate for many thousands of years. Within their rigidity they have expanded, become flexible to accommodate to the needs of more highly evolved civilizations and societies. The basic foundation remains unchanged, it is only the scope that broadens and expands.

It was totally to this purpose that the Ten Commandments were released to the ancient Hebrews. The law is the law, and those who do not follow its path account to themselves for their discretions. We shall see in our journeys through the Bible punishments seemingly meted out to individuals, to families, to nations for laws that have been broken or ignored. You must understand that what befalls mankind he places upon himself, that what occurs to man that is not Godly he has requested.

A soul is created in love, nurtured and developed to grow in love, to become aware in oneness with the I AM. Strive for this in your growth, release those in your lives who prohibit and deter you from finding this Oneness, for this is your destiny, and We Bless you.

Chapter 7

Christos: Questions and Answers

This is Christos. Bless you.

We are going to utilize as much time as necessary tonight to try to update ourselves to the present in our studies by reviewing the first lessons. We shall receive questions relating to anything we have discussed to this point. If there is anything that is not clear, please mention it and we shall discuss it.

Question: Why were the Ten Plagues physical plagues?

Answer: In actuality, if our Father had not interfered the Egyptians would have released the Hebrews after the first plague. However, this was not your Father's Desire. It was desired that both the Egyptians and the Hebrews learn a hard lesson. So, our Father hardened the minds of the Egyptians and gave them the strength to refuse to release the Hebrews. This created a testing situation for the Hebrews relating to their faith in God. The same applied to the Egyptians, for with each ensuing plague the Egyptians steadfastly refused to accept the existence of God until the end.

When the Ten Plagues were over, and the Hebrews left Egypt, our Father once again hardened the minds of the Egyptians. They regretted their action in releasing the Hebrews and gave chase to recapture them. Even though their first-born were slain they still refused to believe in the Lord, and so they died, and so they perished for their total lack of belief in spite of the loss of their beloved.

The ten was a total cycle, a completion and a new beginning, and upon the tenth plague was founded the new beginning, The Exodus.

Question: Were the Pharaoh's priests and ministers avatars?

Answer: I would not say that all of them were avatars. Many of them certainly were. Many of them were from among the Elders of Atlantis there to serve our Father in a positive sense.

Question: During the time of the Ten Plagues when the first-born sons of every Egyptian son was to die, what was meant by "borrowing the child back from God" pertaining to the Hebrews?

Answer: The first-born is considered the seed that perpetuates and carries on the tradition of the family unit. It carries the responsibility for the survival of the aims and purposes of the family. Therefore, it becomes the family's dearest possession.

For this purpose, let us use it as a comparison to Abraham being asked to sacrifice his son, for it was required that every parent understand that their first-born son must be given to their Father as a sign of devotion, as a sign of trust knowing that he is a child of God. It is a symbolic gesture, and yet a highly spiritual one, for it places obligation, responsibilities upon the first-born son to assume a role of leadership in family situations, and a responsibility to his younger siblings. This was very important in those times for their protection and wellbeing.

Question: How does that spiritual law pertain to today?

Answer: The law has indeed changed at this time. Those among the Hebrew religion who practice this law do it because of tradition, and because of their faith and practice of the ancient laws. They still practice the separation and prestige of the eldest son. If it be their truth, then we Bless them for it. Truly the necessity for this type of symbolic sacrifice no longer exists, for in today's awareness and conscious awakening, mankind has come to understand that all are as first-born, that each is an equal child in God's Eyes. This law has softened and expanded as the conscious understanding has developed. In a few words, it is no longer necessary to perform this rite.

Question: In ancient times there was a lot of prostitution. I also know that in the old-time religion if the child was born it was considered to be the same religion as the mother. In the case of a Hebrew female prostitute did this apply, and was the first-born son still offered to God?

Answer: Most definitely so. The law is the law without exception. To this day in the Hebrew religion the child, regardless of the father's religion, is considered to be Hebrew if it is male.

Question: Were the Ten Plagues a direct result of violation of universal law, or were they just tests created by God?

Answer: They were tests created by the Lord for both the Egyptians and the Hebrews. There was great displeasure at the lack of humanitarianism and love shown between these two people. It was intended that they live in peace. It became necessary for both nations to learn a hard, severe lesson.

We must say that, in reality, they brought it upon themselves. We add that the timing for the lessons greatly coincided with certain atmospheric and geographic changes that occurred at that time. The two were not caused by each other, but certainly contributed to each other.

Question: Would you please explain more about the "Spirit Core".

Answer: In the beginning the Divine Essence created a multitude of souls. Over the millennia these souls developed and evolved.

They took to the banks of their energies all that was necessary for them to truly be as spirit, to truly be as One in the vibration with the Divine Essence. When this occurred, the souls resided in the ethers as spirit, and were given the capacity to multiply of themselves not totally, but partially, with a Core always remaining intact. These multiplications occurred in a series of sevens, nine and twelves. Each of these souls repeated through the millennia, themselves, all series of growth and evolvement until they too had reached a point in their growth where they were qualified to serve as spirit' upon reaching Core into divisions of seven, nine and twelve. This process has created a Tree of Life containing all souls that have ever existed throughout Creation. It is why every soul within the confines of Creation carries with it the energies of the Divine Essence, for each is a creation of one created from the Essence. In some instances when a newly created Spirit Core creates of itself the required number of souls, at that point it may assimilate back into the Core that gave birth to it for unified growth at higher levels. That entire Core may move to other galaxies, to other worlds, or to other universes to continue growth at much higher levels of evolvement. This will eventually lead it to the place where it too shall be the Creator of a Universe, and upon that completion assimilate with the Divine Essence for the balance of infinity.

Question: Last week it was stated that after a soul has evolved to a predetermined level, it has a right to end its physical incarnations and assimilate with the Spirit Core. What is the predetermined level?

Answer: Before the spirit divides the Council of Elders, or the Board of Karma predetermines the number of souls to be created from the division and determines the expression of every individual soul. A total pattern of growth and service that the individual soul must undergo in order to complete its "slate" is established. This is why we find within the divisions all of the souls of different quality and texture. Each will have a totally different purpose and a different overall mission for the Father, a different road to walk before it reaches the end. All walk alone yet achieve the same result in the long run. It is necessary to have all these different types of expressions. Without it we would not have societies nor situations to learn, one from the other. Understand that within your conscious life your soul has been guiding you since birth. If your soul is here in love, why has it permitted you, at times, to achieve things improperly and take immoral actions? Many men accumulate wealth by ill-gotten means. Why has the soul permitted this? It is done, for the conscious mind has a strong desire to do so, and therefore, is allowed to take the action and learn from it.

You must experience the wrong to learn the right. If your desires are strong, this shall always occur. Each of us is in a different expression. Each of us walks a different path, and yet in the end they are all as one.

Question: After the soul has reached this predetermined level, you stated that the soul could remain in the present vibrations and be of service to other souls, or it could then go to immediately begin new levels of growth. Could you elaborate on this please?

Answer: I shall try to answer your question within the framework pertaining to this planet. The statement you are referring to basically applies to those souls whom we have referred to as "alien souls", those souls who are here in a series of service incarnations at a lower vibration. When their pattern is completed, they are free of their service contract with our Father and can elect to either stay in the vibrations of this planet to serve as a spiritual master, or to continue their progress and growth at much higher vibrations to achieve things beyond your comprehension.

This may involve other worlds millions of miles away.

Question: When a Spirit Core divides into seven, nine or twelve, do they all incarnate a t the same time, or would they necessarily be on the same planet?

Answer: Upon the creation from the division of spirit all the souls will incarnate together for the first time only. This will usually occur on the same planet, or in the same general area. At that point each one is free, each has the capacity to grow and learn at its own rate. Therefore, the joint pattern of incarnation is broken. No soul is held back for the lack of another's growth. It is very rare to find a soul group of the same spirit incarnating together time after time. This would signify that they have achieved the same levels of growth during a particular incarnation. This rarely happens.

Certain souls within a group will complete their patterns earlier than others, much earlier than others. There a r e times during a series of incarnations when several will elect to incarnate together for a joint mission to band their energies together for a specific purpose. This is occurring in great numbers at this time on Earth, for there is much unification of energies needed to complete the work at this time. This is why there is so much recognition with so many Children of Light.

Question: Is the predetermined level of vibration the point where the superconscious, the conscious and the subconscious become one?

Answer: Generally speaking, this is true. When the individual has come to the point where the three levels of consciousness are as one, and there is total acceptance of the Christ energies within at all levels, then the individual had indeed accepted his capacity for total Love. The only, shall we say, fly in the ointment is once accepting it, has the individual developed the capacity to practice it. This is truly the predetermining factor.

Acceptance is one thing. Utilizing it is sometimes another story.

Question: After one reaches this predetermined level can the soul elect to proceed to areas of higher learning?

Answer: Definitely so. Tere are many souls walking the face of this planet that have spent millions of billions of years in far more highly civilizes Light Worlds, Star Worlds, Quasar Worlds and other types of civilizations. The evolutionary process is extremely complex, and in its complexity is very basic. Understand that when we talk to you of great periods of time, we are using terminology relating to your time frame and time span. The correlation between spiritual time and Earth time has a great degree of variance, for we deal totally in vibrations within our framework of time.

Question: Am I correct in saying that in order to finish your pattern of incarnation your level of growth must be quite high?

Answer: All souls must learn and assimilate the vibrations of Divine Love. While the roads they travel are different, they all must end up at the same place and level of vibration before completion. The various roads create the lessons for interrelating with other people. If every path were the same, no one would learn anything.

Question: Could you elaborate on the definition of spiritual fidelity?

Answer: The "Law of Spiritual Fidelity" basically relates to the statement, "Thou shalt have no other Gods before Me." This means that you shall not commit spiritual adultery by worshipping idols, by worshipping money, cars, men or women, by worshipping anything. Spiritual fidelity is the recognition that your Father is your only true reality Any variance from that truth is spiritual infidelity, for it means a lack of acceptance of the Lord. It is one of the most specific of spiritual law, without leeway, and without room for change.

Question: I want to go back to when we said that the calendar was composed of ten months. If we assume that, we have 280 days which is precisely the term of pregnancy from conception to birth. This seems to be exciting. May I have a comment on this?

Answer: There is truly not much to discuss for you have said it and said it properly. The comment we wish to make is this too is part of the evolutionary process of this planet. The basic stability of the lunar months still exists. It is only the span of the years that has been extended. This is why there is a great variance within the old ancient ten-month calendar, and the one currently using twelve months, for it gives us far fewer years. The cycle of 280 days is indeed a cycle, a completed cycle and corresponds with the cycle of gestation. This is not a coincidence.

Question: Is there any other reason for an alien soul to incarnate on Earth than to do service?

Answer: The only other purpose for an alien soul to incarnate within a sphere of a lower vibration would be as the result of a circumstance involving the necessity for a relearning process for something not utilized properly, or greatly misused. Under normal conditions this will not occur. We could use as an example the situation where a soul has committed suicide during an incarnation and must return to relearn lessons not learned.

Question: Some time ago we were told that the vibrations of this planet will change shortly. Can you elaborate on this for us?

Answer: As does a soul, each planet has a destiny, for planets are not created by accident; they are all part of the Divine Plan of creation and evolution. As the soul evolves so must the vibrations of the planet it is inhabiting. If not, it would have to incarnate elsewhere, finding a planet whose vibrations are compatible with those of the soul. When this occurs on Earth those who have not grown will be forced to continue their evolution on other planets that are compatible with their level of vibrations.

We must now end the session for tonight. We Bless you in Love.

Chapter 8

The Father: "Sin" and "Guilt"

These are the energies of your Father, and I Bless you, My Children.

Due to the nature of the topic for tonight's discussion, I have chosen to send My Energies to you, for it is of a most serious nature.

We talk tonight of a much maligned, much misunderstood word. The word is SIN. The Book of Leviticus contains a category of paragraphs describing lists of many sins that man commits, or committed, and the penance or punishment assigned to each particular sin. For many centuries mankind has lived in fear, not so much in fear of what they considered to be God, but more in fear of what they considered to be sin without even bothering to find out what the word meant and where it had its origin.

Historians refer to the original sin in the symbolism of Eve biting the apple of forbidden fruit. Was this a sin, or was it symbolically freedom of choice? If you are to sit here and say that Eve had no right to take a bite of the apple, are you not judging? Can you say that if perhaps you were in her shoes, you might not also have tasted of the so-called "forbidden fruit"?

Man says that the Master Jesus died on the cross for all the sins of mankind. Did this relieve man of his obligations to his Father? Did this free man from his lessons of growth and experience? Most assuredly not. What sins did Jesus then die for? If man truly needs to have a sin, then let there only be one, and let that one be a lack of belief in God. For if indeed I AM is your only reality, and all else is a projection in constant change, then that can be the only sin.

Is it a sin to steal? Or is it a free will decision that draws to the individual a severe lesson, the lesson being of a nature of the individual's own choosing.

The Bible talks of the vengeance of the Lord. Throughout periods of history, it has been said that I have "smitten" those who have sinned, that I have hurled tempests and floods and bolts of lightning to punish man. There is a passage which states, "Vengeance is Mine, sayeth the Lord." My energies are energies of Divine Love. Those who err in their ways draw to them their own justice, bring to themselves their own degree of lesson. They know at the soul level the degree of vibration they have misused, and the degree of balancing vibration that is necessary to once again restore the equilibrium. This is universal law. The word vengeance does not exist, for if it did exist the Energies of your Father would not be a constant, but a variable, and your world would be in total chaos.

Why then did the sages, the ancient Rabbis, put so much stress on the word "sin"? The people were weak, their minds and their truth vacillated from day to day. There was a need for a weapon, a weapon to bind the people together. They chose to accomplish this with fear. The fear they chose to hold the people together was the word "sin".

Why did I allow this to occur? Why did I not stop this at its inception? It was the choice of the leaders to take this action. I did not wish to interfere. The free will of man must be given exercise and freedom. If not, he shall not grow. Even in this present day many of you when you were children were taught to be in fear of sin and have had to work diligently to overcome this stigma, this limit on your freedom of expression.

In the Bible it states that if a man stole another man's sheep, he had sinned and would be severely punished for this act. There are lists of sins which call for the loss of a hand, a foot, the loss of eyesight, the loss of a tongue and other punishments. Does this sound like a Father speaking to a child in Love, or does it sound like retribution in the form of an eye for an eye, and a tooth for a tooth?

It states in Leviticus that if one commits a sin without knowing that the act was sinful, he still must bear punishment for the sin. How could this be? Was this perhaps written as a deterrent? You know that any action that is taken in your truth is not sinful, draws to you no lesson, and is only an experience for you. If you are unaware of the proper course of action due to lack of exposure to this situation, then you are accountable to yourself to learn, to learn from the experience so that it shall not occur again.

The laws relating to sin in the Book of Leviticus do not pertain to mankind at this present time. If it were possible to erase the word, sin, wherever it is written and replace it with the word, lesson, I would ask that it be done. Man has evolved to the point where he no longer needs to relate to his Father's Energies in fear. He can relate openly in love and accept his mistakes. The Hebrews celebrate the holiday called, "Yom Kippur", it is the day of atonement, the holiest day of the year. It is a day when forgiveness is asked for a twenty-four-hour period for all the sins that have been committed during the course of the year. They are listed and categorized, many tens of them. Within each sentence is the word, sin. Forgiveness is asked for those sins they have not even consciously committed, just in case.

Man does not need to grovel on his knees before his Father. It is much preferred that he sits in meditation and feel the presence of his Father within, to sense the freedom, the lack of guilt, the understanding of self. Let him know that his existence is free, guided by the energies of Divine Love, by the energies of Divine Oneness so that all may grow and experience in truth.

Read part of the Book of Leviticus, and where you come to the part where the word "sin" is written, substitute the word "lesson", for it will change your reaction to many passages that you read. When a man says, "I have sinned," whom is he referring to? For if he has sinned, obviously he has sinned against someone. Does he feel that he has "sinned" against God, or does he feel that he has "sinned" against himself? Most times man feels that he has "sinned" against God. In truth he has "sinned" against himself, or he has taken an action in his life that he knew was not his truth, and therefore has decided that he must learn from it and must take a counteraction to rectify his mistake.

I am not even involved in this type of action. I am only involved when you deny My Existence. The solution to the problem of sin is quite simple. If you will take the step forward and accept My Presence within you and accept My Guidance in all facets of your life, you never need be concerned, for you shall know that you are walking in truth and love. All your actions and your decisions shall be taken in "Our" vibrations, for at that moment We shall be as One, and Our Purpose and Actions shall be as One. ' You need never again concern yourselves with the energies that are called "sin".

Is the word "guilt" synonymous with the word "sin"? In many ways it is. What causes guilt? Inadequacy, a lack of strength within your faith and your convictions? Perhaps it is making your decisions too quickly resulting in second thoughts that allow you to feel guilty for the choice you have made. Once having decided that you are guilty you might as well say that you have "sinned".

You have no right to "guilt". You have no right to regret an action. You must take your actions only when they are your truth, and if you cannot determine which course of action is your truth, postpone the action until you can.

The time has arrived for mankind to release the energies of self-punishment and lack of self-worth. He must stand strong and firm. He must move forward in a positive direction and recognize that he is an instrument of love and love alone.

I do not wish to be related to by man in fear. I do not wish to be related to in awe. I wish only to be related to in love. These are the Words I speak to you tonight, My Children. Ponder them carefully and seriously, for within them is a solution to a most important part of your growth and your peace. Walk in freedom and walk in love. I Bless you all.

This is Christos. Bless you.

If anyone has any questions relating to the words spoken to you by your Father, I shall be glad to discuss them with you at this time.

Questions and Answers

Question: We have learned that an action brings on energies in the exact opposite direction. If someone sins will that bring them to the opposite energies?

Answer: It is a variable. There are times when a person who incurs a lesson will experience the exact energies to learn the lesson from. However, the energies in the opposite and equal direction are created and may be utilized by someone else involved in the same category of lesson. It truly depends upon the person's willingness and understanding of the lesson. Many times, it is felt that the opposite expression will be best to learn the lesson from. In those instances, the lesson will generally be more severe. So, it will depend upon the severity of the lesson in most cases.

Question: It is my understanding that what you send out returns to you in like whether you are aware of it or not. Yet I have heard it said that one does not draw karma if they are unaware of an action. Could you explain the distinction here?

Answer: If I send you vibrations of hate, they shall return to me tenfold, for I know that the vibrations of hate are not "true" vibrations, they are vibrations of my own creation. The only true vibrations are those of love. For that reason, I would draw to myself a lesson, if I send you out vibrations of love, the love shall return to me tenfold, for I would have given of myself to you, and it would return to me in like.

If you commit an act of violence, or take a detrimental action against me, and I send you energies in love, it shall be recognized within your vibrations that you have erred, and you shall draw to yourself a lesson to relearn. If you take this action against me, and I send you negativity, you shall not become aware of your error, for it shall return to me. So, you are doing a service when you send someone love who has erred against you, for you are allowing them to recognize that they have made a mistake and are giving them the opportunity to rectify it. Otherwise, you are acknowledging their action as truth, for you are returning like energies.

Question: Are separate lessons learned by the soul and the personality?

Answer: This is absolutely true. Many times, people wonder why someone takes a particular action feeling that the soul must have known it was the wrong thing to do. But there is the Law of Free Will, and if the conscious personality has a strong enough desire to take an action, the soul will step aside for the growth of the personality. This will occur even though the soul knows that the course of action is not the proper one. All is geared at the soul level to eventually blend with the consciousness as one. If the conscious mind is strong enough to overcome the intuitive thoughts placed there by the soul, to insist on taking its own action, it can do so. Many times, we find lessons pertaining to the consciousness that are not lessons of the soul.

Question: If this is true, then how does the personality that I am now utilize skills that the soul has learned through other personalities, and how will the personality that I will be in the future learn the lessons that I have acquired in this life?

Answer: The progression is that the personality does not survive after the physical passing. It is only the knowledge and experiences that are assimilated into the energy banks of the soul. The emotional aspects of the personality become null and void, and with each ensuing incarnation it is only the knowledge and experience that is available to that conscious personality during that specific incarnation. The expression of it positively or negatively becomes the choice of the consciousness during the incarnation. The emotional reaction to that experience in the past no longer exists.

We shall now end this portion of tonight's class. We Bless you in our Father's Name.

Chapter 9

Toran: Pre-Biblical Civilizations on Earth.

Good evening and Bless you. My name is Toran.

In your language it would be spelled, Toran. My energies have come here from beyond the confines of this Universe. It is a most difficult adjustment, so if the speech seems to falter, please understand.

I have been called upon by the Divine Creator to speak with you this night to relay to you information pertaining to pre-biblical days and times regarding this planet. What I say to you now has never been said in the history of current civilization.

Many, many millions of years ago five highly advanced, superior forms of life existed upon the surface of this planet. This may seem to be in direct opposition to what you have been taught relating to vibrations and compatibility. However, the civilizations were enclosed with walls of energy to contain their own vibration levels. This enabled them to exist on this planet. They were in the form of an experimental task force to help establish patterns of energy to help determine the feasibility for karmic incarnation on this planet.

We are going to describe the civilizations for you. The first to arrive came in a fleet of ships that traveled several hundred years to reach this planet. They came from the planet, "Zorg", six hundred and seventy-four light years away from this planet. They were embodied in a physical structure reaching a height of approximately seven feet tall. They were extremely thin with oversize cranial structures. Their feet contained heavy padding and were webbed for greater stability and maneuverability.

The second civilization came from the planet, "Ralur", over a million light years away from Earth. Their physical structures averaged four feet in height. They were of stocky build with oversize cranial structures.

The third civilization came from the planet, "Arlom". It is located two hundred thousand light years away from Earth.

Their height averaged five feet. Their bodies were lean. They possessed antenna that protruded from the top of their heads. Their hands and feet were also webbed.

The fourth civilization came from the planet, "Urali", located at the far outer limits of this galaxy. They were totally androgenous beings. Their physical structure bore no resemblance to your male and female structure of today.

The fifth civilization came from the planet, "Poral". Their height averaged over eight feet tall. Their physical structures were massive, highly muscular.

And so, we had five varied forms of beings incarnated on this planet as test groups. They were to determine the proper types of characteristics necessary for inhabitation on Earth. They were to determine the proper mode of physical structure along with all other physical characteristics.

The five civilizations migrated for many millions of years, shuttling from one geographical location to another, determining factors, selecting areas for habitation, and establishing energy conditions. They altered patterns of energy flows to assist in establishing climactic conditions conducive to habitation. They assisted in the breeding of various forms of prehistoric animals and marine forms of life.

It is important for you to understand that these civilizations were extremely highly evolved and capable of achieving and performing things to a degree far beyond your comprehension at this time.

We wish you to know that the earliest forms of recorded human-oid incarnations on this planet came long after these alien beings had arrived, stayed, and departed from this planet. Do not for a moment conceive that you are descended from ancient cavemen or Neanderthal creatures, for this is not true. Within each millen-nia a strata of incarnation assumed form on this planet in the proper level of vibrations. They existed, survived, and became ex-tinct when compatibility with the vibrations on the planet ceased to exist. This made way for more highly evolved forms of struc-tures, more advanced groups of souls to incarnate and proceed with their patterns of growth.

During the reign of the experimental civilizations land masses were shifted. Tremendous earth changes occurred to establish a flowing balance and create harmony of vibrations. Periodically throughout history this has occurred again and again as a read-justment to rising levels of vibrations to maintain this balance.

Why have I come and related this to you? The things that I have said occurred long before the Bible you are discussing was written. It is important for you to understand the foundation on which so-called modern civilizations have been structured and built. Would it surprise you if I said that there shall be another Bible written in the beginning of the Twenty-First Century? It shall relate to the re-awakening of the Messiah. Please take note. I did not say reincar-nation, I said re-awakening, for mankind shall be the Messiah.

The new Bible, when it shall be written, shall be complete. It shall contain descriptions of Creation, the evolution of this planet, and many facts and areas not covered in the

present volumes as written. Who knows, since you shall all be here at that time perhaps some of you will take a hand in the writing of this manuscript and place your mark on history.

It is almost time for me to leave, but before I depart, I have a message for you all from the Creator. Treasure this being through whom I speak. He cannot hear my words, for the first time he is not in control of what is being channeled through him. He is an instrument of great truth and power.

I take your leave now, and I charge you with the responsibility of your growth, and I charge you with the responsibility to lead your lives in God's Work and for your fellow man. I say to you, "Solaris Thoris", which means on your planet, Shalom.

The Father: The Law of Prosperity

These are the Energies of your Father, My Children, and I Bless you.

I wish to speak to you tonight on the law pertaining to greed. We talk of the Laws of Prosperity. We talk of the Law of Substance and Flow. We are all aware that in order for the Law of Prosperity to function properly it is necessary to continue the flow unbroken, not to erect a dam in the stream to stem the flow of the water, but to keep the stream free from debris so the flow may continue uninterrupted. Periodically one comes along who builds a dam and the name of the dam is "greed". Greed is not confined alone to involvements with money. It is involved with property and estate, with animals and other possessions. It is involved within personalities, for people conceive in their minds that they possess people. So, we find that the greatest offense that we label greed is involved in the interrelationship of people. It occurs when we do not allow freedom of expression for those whom we love and share our lives with. We wish to hold onto them in our mold and thought patterns, for our own insecurities prevent us from allowing them their own expression. We do this out of fear lest we lose them. In doing so we stop the flow, and we cause agitation and resentment and blockages. Our lives become stifled, and our growth is slowed considerably.

The man who walks with his Father, who unites his energies with his Father's Love need never suffer frustrations and anxieties and has no cause to become involved in the energies of greed. So, the substance flows smoothly to and from, and to again.

This universal law never varies. It is a constant. How many do you know who have hoarded out of greed, who have retained what they have hoarded and not lost it all in time? In essence, they have denied their Oneness with their Father, for they have not trusted in His Flow of Substance.

Throughout your readings in the Bible there are examples time and time again pointing to lack of faith in flow. It resulted in severe hardships. What would have happened if Pharaoh would have released the Hebrews at Moses' first request, if he would have had faith that God's Will be done instead of holding onto the supply at hand, the supply of labor and slaves? Egypt would have continued to flourish instead of undergoing devastation and ruin for many, many years.

This example has been repeated time and time again. Look at your world as it exists for you now with nation upon nation striving to amass munitions and hold onto positions of power instead of releasing and allowing to flow. The greatest greed involves the greed towards self, the unwillingness of man to release himself to his Father's Care but insists on holding on to what he thinks he possesses in the way of material things and emotional attachments.

So, I say to you, My Children, you who strive to become enlightened, to become one with self, have the faith, release yourself to Me. You shall not fall. You shall rise, and your flow of substance shall continue to grow and increase.

This is My Message for you this evening, My Children, and I Bless you and wish you continued success in your evolvement.

Chapter 10

Toran: Questions Relating to Ancient Civilizations

Bless you and good evening. This is Toran speaking.

It is my pleasure to once again bring my energies to this Circle of Light. During this past week I am sure all of you have noticed a change in your vibrational structure. This change shall increase as time goes on.

We would like to use this session to answer any questions that may have arisen out of last week's transmission. Please proceed.

Question: Those from other planets who have physical bodies that are so different from ours, do they have any physical similarities to our physical structures on any other planets?

Answer: There are many civilizations where the physical structure is quite similar to yours. Some where it is almost identical. But, in the infinite truth, there are no two that are exactly the same. The conditions, the energies, the structures of atmosphere and other things related to civilizations determine the form of structure that can be utilized. Understand that the physical vehicle is merely a tool. Its total purpose is to carry the soul, and to enable the conscious individual to function in the structure of a society, and to survive in that existence.

Those of the Ancients all possessed different physical structures. This was intentionally done to help ascertain the type of physical structure most suitable for this planet.

Question: Could you tell us more about the planet Urali? You said that the beings were androgenous. What was the purpose of the planet, and what was the philosophy of the civilization?

Answer: In stating that the beings were androgenous, we might rephrase the statement to say that they were, from an energy standpoint totally in balance. They were capable of manifesting themselves in either male or female condition to suit their purposes at any given time. It is not necessary for me to tell you that the soul in spirit form is, of course, totally androgenous. This denotes a high level of development and evolution for these souls.

The structure of their civilization on their native planet was, you might say, compared to a finishing school. The civilization is very highly advanced. Most of their work and effort is involved within other civilizations and planets and worlds. They help other children grow and develop. On their native planet their normal state is in energy form, although for their purposes of travel to other planets they do assume physical form. The physical form they assumed on this planet was not necessarily the form they would assume somewhere else. It would depend on the conditions that existed on the particular planet. Many times, they have totally assimilated within a society so as to be unnoticed to perform their work from within the society.

Questions and Answers

Question: Are any of these beings working with us now?

Answer: Generally speaking, no. There are a few exceptions. Most of the work that is being done from these lost civilizations is being done through energy waves rather than through the actual presence of the soul on Earth. But there are some of these beings that are here at this present time.

Question: The many different types of bodies they assume, is it possible that some of the remains our scientists have found of large, oversize creatures could be some of these Ancients?

Answer: This is absolutely true.

Question: This was so long ago. Could the legends of the giants go back so far?

Answer: Some of the legends relating to the giant civilizations are pertaining to societies that lived at a much later period in time, not necessarily to the earliest ones. What is known commonly as the Yeti is the remains of a lost civilization that settled here on Earth from space. It is true that several of them still exist and walk this planet.

Question: Are there any Yeti on this continent?

Answer: Yes, there are several to be found in the northern most part of the United States bordering on Canada, more into Canada than the United States. Generally speaking, their bodily functions and systems need the cold to survive. They could not survive in your city of Phoenix. Their metabolism is very slow. This also gives them their long span of life. Many of them are several hundred years old.

Question: Are they still performing a function as a highly evolved spiritual soul?

Answer: They are serving in a capacity as energy transfer points. Although the average man on Earth would consider them ignorant in a cultural sense, their minds and their spiritual attunement are extremely highly evolved. They serve to cleanse an area of nega-tivity, and to keep energy channels open and clear. This is their prime function at this time.

In approximately one hundred and fifty years they shall no longer be seen on this planet.

Question: In terms of what we call Earth years, would you please give us some ideas as to how old you are?

Answer: I would be approximately 347 trillion of your years old.

Question: Are you consciously aware of the time when the planet Earth began forming?

Answer: Truthfully, I must say no. You must understand that Creation is quite vast. Universes are being created and destroyed even as we talk. There was no special need or purpose for me to be aware of the creation of this Universe over the creation of any other one. So, there was no special attention by me when it was created.

Question: Is there a prescribed progression of incarnation for all souls?

Answer: When a soul assumes its very first incarnation, it is only for a span ranging between twelve to eighteen of your years. It involves a series of from twelve to sixteen incarnations on that planet. The vibrations on that planet are very elementary and very basic, for the prime function is for the soul to acclimate itself to physical incarnation, and to be involved within its karmic pattern. When the soul has reached the desired level of growth, it will elect to incarnate for a second series on a planet whose vibrations are at a slightly higher level, offering it exposure to additional growth. This is the process that is repeated tens of thousands of times with each ensuing series of incarnations being assumed on a planet with higher and higher vibrations.

There is no set pattern or schedule of planets to incarnate on. The soul has the leeway to elect the galaxy or solar system that will afford it the opportunity to work out its pattern for an upcoming incarnation. Be aware that it is very rare for a soul to assume a single incarnation on a planet. The series normally will last anywhere from twelve to sixty or seventy. It will depend on the area of growth that is desired.

I must add that there are indeed a great quantity of highly evolved souls incarnated on your planet at this time doing service for the Divine Creator. Even in their case the law is the law, and many of them had to assume a total series of incarnations to fit into the pattern of energies so as not to break the flow and break the continuity of vibrations. There are some who have been here for only a short while, but this is the exception, not the rule.

Question: What is the relationship of the Father to the Divine Creator?

Answer: The word, Father, is used in many different connotations. Are you using the word, Father, in relation to the Trinity associated with your planet? ("I am referring to That which channels through Frank.") I must say that they are one and the same.

Question: what is this relationship to the One you refer to as the Divine Creator?

Answer: It is just two ways of expressing the same thing.

Question: when you become One with the Father do you become One with the Creator of this Universe, or One with the Creator of all?

Answer: The first step of the progression is to become One with the Father of the Universe that you are existing in. When the time comes that you are One with the Divine Creator that is the time when total assimilation takes place. You then are as He, your lessons and service have been completed, and it is time for you to assimilate back into your source. At that moment you become One with the Divine Creator totally. Man's purpose here is to become One with the soul you call God, or Father of this Universe, the Creator of this Universe. This must be done in order for your energies at the spirit level to break free of the pattern of energies of this Universe. Without this Oneness,

it is impossible for you to advance beyond the confines of this Universe. You would be held within this Universal vibration until that time.

Question: For what purpose do the highly evolved souls here do astral traveling?

Answer: The prime purpose and function of astral traveling is to help others in their work, to lend assistance when necessary. In the pure sense astral traveling, or energy projections as we prefer to call it, is used to assist in energy buildup if it is required somewhere in the world.

The energies are projected to that area to assist in the project or function.

The visual perception that many people receive from astral projection is merely a by-product of the function. It rarely bears any significance to the true purpose.

Question: Is there any significance to the fact that my name in my next incarnation will be the same as the ancient civilization called Poral?

Answer: It is not a coincidence for the level of vibrations within your soul to bear a strong correlation to this ancient civilization. For your general information, let me add this: during the last incarnation on a planet the individual will carry almost the total vibrations of the soul consciously from birth. This will enable that individual to ascertain its purpose from a young age, and to avoid any distortion of the purpose and path for the incarnation. The path of the life is more closely defined, and the individual is strongly directed to the fulfillment of its mission.

Many individuals assume at the conscious level the name that is the expression of their souls, so both are called as one. This signifies a oneness of vibrations and helps to augment this oneness.

Question: To what planet will those souls who will not evolve as the vibrations of the planet Earth change, incarnate on?

Answer: They shall be divided among three planets. I have been advised that it is not proper to give you the names and locations of these planets at this time. But what I shall say is this: within two of the planets the civilizations are almost on a par with the civilizations on Earth now. The third planet carries a slightly lower structure of energies and shall be populated by those who need to continue to work on important parts of their karmic patterns.

Question: Once the vibrations of the Earth will change, what will the lifestyle here be like?

Answer: The life patterns shall change quite slowly. There shall be much turmoil. Let us talk of the time when the change has been completed, when the battle of Armageddon has subsided.

At that time there shall never again be a war on this planet. There will be no need for defense budgets or munitions plants, for the world shall slowly become a world of love. There shall be a strong return to an agrarian form of life, for the world shall be deeply involved in ecology, conservation, health and proper diet.

There will be much resistance at first, but in the end, man shall recognize his brothers and sisters, and people shall stop calling themselves Christians and Jews and Moslems, and allow themselves to be in total brotherhood, to recognize the universal spirituality of God without the restricting labels, labels of division rather than those of unity. The key word shall be unity at all levels.

It is going to begin with the children. You shall find in the next decade spiritual centers of learning that will be designed for the education and growth of children. The reprogramming of the parents will take too much time. The future is with the children.

The road for what I have described to you is not smooth. There will be many stumbling blocks and failures on the path to success, but in the end, there will be success, for this is how it must be.

We take your leave at this time. There shall be a pause in the communication for a few moments for he shall experience the infusion of new energies once again this night, and we Bless you.

Dianne

Bless you. I am indeed a female expression, but as we are using his vocal chords you will have to overlook the texture of his voice.

I come to you nameless, but you may call me Dianne, as I come to you and present myself to you as Love. I am not here to give you a lecture or a dissertation. I am here to have you enjoy an experience. I am here to make my Love available to all of you now, and whenever you may have a need for it in the future.

If you wish, you may say that I bring you the energies of the Mother. So, if you will all close your eyes, I shall touch you all and bring you your Mother's Love so that it may be with you always....

It has been said that an action is better than a thousand words, and so I have shared with you my Love and my vibrations. It shall serve for the lecture that I have not given. I am here to prepare you for the times of stress ahead. I am here to establish a connecting link between us so that in times of stress you may draw upon my Love for strength, and to restore your vibrations to their normal levels. We have now touched and shared, and when you have a need for me in the future, I shall always be available to you. I take your leave, and I Bless you one and all.

Chapter 11

Toran: Early Humanoid Forms.

Good evening and Bless you. This is Toran.

We are going to discuss some of the purposes and obligations that man assumed when he chose incarnation on this planet. He has, of course, as one of his main obligations his growth and development. But he has also assumed obligations to his Father. He must recognize his Father's eternal existence and know that the Father is with him at all times, and that there is no other but He. It sounds very simple, and indeed it is. Yet, in its simplicity it is quite complex, for the tools made available to man to achieve this recognition have varied greatly throughout history.

Let us take a trip back into time many billions of years ago, approximately fourteen billion years ago when some of the first humanoid structures incarnated on this planet. We are going back to a time prior to the time discussed several weeks ago relating to the five civilizations we described for you.

The earliest humanoid forms did not bear too much resemblance to yourselves. Their life span was no longer than twenty or twenty-five of your years. The physical beings embodied a soul at a much lower level of evolution than yours. The earliest beings were created devoid of what you refer to as the five senses: those of sight, hearing, taste, smell and speech.

It is passing through your minds, "how could this be, for they would be like lost sheep." Indeed, they were. They were no more than slightly elevated above the highest animal strata of life. They did not walk erect, for they used their hands to help them find their way on the ground. Any form of communication was accomplished at a basic sensory level. In time it was decided that this type of incarnation would not suffice, and when the souls assigned to incarnation here in their own rudimentary level achieved a level of growth, the first of five senses appeared, the sense of sight. Over the millennia the other senses were granted to mankind one by one. To this day they are still being granted to mankind at more and more sensitive levels.

The animal life during those early years did not exist in the form known to man as prehistoric animals. All was at an extremely rudimentary level consisting of different forms of bacteria and single cell organisms that existed, for the most part, in the waters. The people sustained themselves from various roots, berries, and other forms of vegetation that grew around them.

I wish to tell you at this time that there are other civilizations in this and other universes existing at the level I am describing to you at this time. We must always keep in the front of our minds the compatibility factors of energy, knowing that we can only have a soul incarnating on a planet whose growth is compatible with the vibrations of that planet. If it were possible for science to record some sort of time structure depicting when energy levels changed on this planet, we would have a much truer picture of civilization structure and evolution. It would give accurate time periods for different levels of civilizations.

Now I am going to turn the balance of tonight's class back to my dear brother Moses who has patiently sat aside for several weeks to that I may share with you. I wish to say that I have visited with several of you this past week and shall be with more of you as time progresses. Bless you.

Moses: The Law of Acquisition

Bless you, my children. There are the energies of Moses.

I am extremely pleased at your progress, and to the extent you have absorbed the information that has been presented to you these past several weeks.

I wish to talk to you tonight on a very personal level relating things to you about myself so that perhaps you, and others who may read my words in the future shall gain some insight into themselves, and perhaps achieve a measure of assistance within their own growth and path. I do not believe that I was what you call a strong man, not speaking from the physical sense but speaking from a spiritual sense. My life was basically full of doubts many times expressed in a lack of faith, not so much a lack of faith in our Father as a lack of faith in my ability to accomplish what He desired me to do.

Too many times during my trails I asked the Lord, "Why me?", far too many times. Those words, "why me", denote a lack of faith in self in the acceptance of, and the release to the God within, causing fears and doubts and apprehensions.

When our Father called to me to ascend the mountain to receive His Laws, and I walked up that mountain shrouded in fog so thick that I could hardly see, I was very much a frightened human being. I had no idea what awaited me at the summit. I had no idea if I would ever return, and I sat and I waited and I waited for our Father to appear. I did not understand why He was not there to greet me upon my arrival, for if He had summoned me then surely, He must be there, and yet He was not.

I never understood until my incarnation had ended, and the realization of what was being done came to my awareness. The waiting had been a personal test of myself in my faith in my Father. I have asked myself many times since then, "what would have occurred if I had decided not to wait and had run down the mountain? Where would the world be today?" The answer is, of course, exactly where it is, for in time I would have been brought back up the mountain.

When our Father finally appeared to me and handed me His Laws, they were all ready for me. There are versions of history that relate different stories. Some say that- I carved tablets out of rock and carved His Laws on the tablets. Others say that giant thunderbolts of lightening carved the words in the tablets. In actuality they were there waiting for me, complete, lying on the ground.

The tablets were far too heavy for me to carry, for I was not a young man. If I had been a young man, I still could not have borne them, and yet I did. They seemed to me to weigh as a feather. They were tablets of Light and Love, and truly were not a burden to carry but a joy.

When I reached the bottom of the mountain and saw what the people had done, I was ashamed and enraged. I judged them one and all and took the tablets of Love and smashed them on the ground. At that moment I felt as if I was a lost soul, for in my heart I did not wish to go back up the mountain, but I did. I went to receive another set of tablets to bring down to God's children without judgment.

The lessons I learned from the incarnation as Moses stood me in great stead in several future incarnations. As we will progress through history, we shall discuss some of them, in particular King David and Caesar Agustus.

At this time, I wish to make clear for you the association and correlation between Toran and myself, for there is indeed a connection there. It was he, following the instructions of the Divine Creator, who brought to me during my incarnation as Moses much of the truths and information that comprise what is known as the Kabbala.

The world is moving closer and closer to the time when this truth shall be revealed in its original undistorted meaning and vibrations. It shall not come to pass until we here are assured that the truth shall be accepted as such and shall be utilized properly for humanity and for growth.

There is an area that is somewhat distasteful to discuss but is necessary to discuss. Many of you are familiar to some degree with mythological creatures that were half-man, half beast. This was not mythology, it was reality. It came close in proportion to being quite a problem, for within an era in ancient times when man turned from his Father and lead a carnal life, sodomy was rampant. Many of the ancient Elders achieved conception with animals creating many forms of mutations. It required vast epidemics of disease to rid the planet of these mutations, for the type and structure of these creatures was not desired nor part of the Divine Plan.

Understand that they were real. They truly did exist. You all sit here today and consider yourselves civilized and advanced beings. In many aspects this is true. Some of the civilizations from the past conducted themselves and their lifestyles in manners which would turn you away in disgust.

Yet for them in their level of growth the reaction to that way of life could not be as yours, and so we must not judge them.

I want to spend a few moments talking to you about what is known as the "Law of Acquisition". The law states quite simply that anyone may acquire what they have determined is a need for them to any degree or quantity as long as it is acquired in good faith, honorably, and through their own efforts.

Out of all of our Father's Laws perhaps this one has been the most difficult to observe. Man has consistently given himself to the feelings of unworthiness, to the feelings of poverty and other negative energies. The time has come for all to understand that it is not your Father's Desire that you be deprived of anything in order to prove your devotion to Him, or to achieve your spiritual growth. It is not necessary for one to incur suffering upon oneself, to feel pain and anguish to grow, to feel deprivation to grow, or to feel unworthiness to grow. All we must feel is our Father within.

The ancients tore their clothes and covered themselves with ashes upon the loss of a loved one. This is done to this day in many areas of religious practice. Why should they not rejoice at the return of a child to spirit? They felt it made them better men to suffer so. They felt it brought them closer to their Father to suffer and bring misery upon themselves. They stripped themselves of their possessions. The Holy Men were beggars without assets, wandering from place to place, depending upon the charity of others for their sustenance. This was not proper. This is not the way your Father intends it to be. There is to be joy in your growth. There is to be joy in your acquisition, spiritually as well as physically.

The suffering that man endures is a manifestation of his own creation to prove his unworthiness to himself. Why? Let man prove his worth, not his lack of worth, for only then can he achieve. Under the Law of Acquisition things acquired in the proper manner and by the proper methods continue to flow in and out, always being replenished, always being passed on to others. When things are acquired in violation of the law, the flow stops, suffering endures, deprivation eventually occurs, for it is a sign of lack of faith.

Raise your sights in your lives. Do not bend and stoop your shoulders. Do not humble yourself, for there is no one to humble yourself to, only yourself.

Let us look for a moment at the ancient Hebrew civilization. We can recall several thousand years of suffering. There are those who say the suffering is karmic to repay a debt to the Father. Who decided this? Was it our Father, or was it the people themselves creating their penance and punishment for judging themselves unworthy, for not allowing themselves to acquire their self-worth and their growth? Who is to say?

At this point I take your leave for tonight. I Bless you in the Divine Creator's Name. God Bless you.

Bless you. This is Christos speaking.

I wish to talk to you only for a few moments to inform you that as the weeks shall pass the energies that shall be coming to you shall become more and more intense and deeply involved. Periodically we shall have sessions as we had last week devoted solely to questions. We suggest that you write out your questions each week so that they shall be fresh in your minds.

We are not in a time of superficiality. We must dig deep, perhaps at time to open wounds, but we must uncover the truth. I Bless you.

Chapter 12

Lucifer: His Function for God.

This is your Father speaking to you, My Children. Bless you.

I have prepared for you quite an unusual program this evening. Perhaps what you are about to experience is not directly related to your studies in this class, and yet in the overall perspective it most assuredly is. Christos has agreed to allow a certain vibration of energies to channel through him this night at my request. It is something that is rarely done, but I have assured him that he and all of you are protected and need have nothing to fear now, and after the session has ended. And so, without further ado, I bring you another of My Sons.

I have spoken to Mr. Alper before, and he was not very polite to me and ordered me out of his vibrations. I can understand why. I could have come to you in one of many different ways: a thundering roar, soft and sweet, blessing you, retaining my image or destroying it. I prefer to come to you as I have. I am, of course, the energies of Lucifer, the reigning soul in the negative kingdom, if you wish to put it that way. He has guts, that much I'll say for him. I don't know anyone else who would allow me to do this.

Why am I here? I am here to destroy some myths about myself, and perhaps to reinforce some other myths. I want you to understand the role I play within the balance of the Universe, within the balance of your lives. You see, I am my Father's Son, and believe it or not, I am not out to destroy my Father. I am not out to destroy your world or the Universe. I am doing my work. I am doing my work as my Father has directed me to do. Should I repeat that for you? I will. I am doing my work as my Father has directed me to do!

Somebody has to be the "bad boy", and I am he. Do I like being the "bad boy"? Sometimes I do not like myself very much, but most of the time I understand the prime purpose for the actions I take. I know what it is I am to help achieve, for without the control of what you call the negative energies the system of karmic incarnation that you are all here under would cease to function.

Sometimes I wish that I could explain to all what my role is, but that is impossible, for if everyone began to like me, I would lose my effectiveness. In your case, our Father asked me to speak to you tonight, and that is why I am here. Someone must understand. Someone must be in a position not to fear me, but to understand that I too am doing our Father's Work, to know that there is a basic function and purpose for what I do.

One of my prime functions relating to your planet is to test, to test the awakened Children of Light to see if their commitment is true and valid, or if they can be swayed from their path. If I can sway them from their path, whether it be with threats, temptations, or promises of greater glories then they are replaced. This is very necessary to determine, for if someone is endowed with great responsibility and power, and if there is a chance that they can be turned from their path by someone or something then that power can become a force for destruction. So, before it is granted to someone your Father must be doubly sure a thousand-fold that nothing can turn them from their path, not even Lucifer.

Some of you have faced me in subtle ways, none as yet directly but you certainly shall in the future. I am not what people refer to as "Satan", residing in a fiery hell, for there is no such place. I am not locked away in the lowest levels of heaven where our Father's

Light does not shine in eternal punishment for bad deeds or sins. This is jibberish designed to put fear into the hearts of mankind to destroy man's free will. I am a free soul such as you with a great responsibility for our Father. It does not matter what the expression is as long as it is a necessary expression for balance and for growth.

When you reject the negativity, I may project to you how do you know that I do not Bless you for your rejection? Even though I may tempt you I still may Bless you when you reject me. If you judge not others, then do not judge me.

Let us go back to some of the earlier lessons in this class you are undertaking to the time of the Ten Plagues when it is written that at the end of a plague when Moses asked the Pharaoh to release the people, that the Lord hardened the Pharaoh's heart so that he would not let them go. That was not our Father directly, that was I at our Father's Orders and Directions. I was offering Pharaoh my negativity, my power, greed, and riches. I turned his mind, so much so that he allowed his people to continue to suffer for his own greed.

This is only one example of the utilization of "temptation energies" if you wish to call them that. They have been expressed and tested time and time again throughout history. Whenever any one of you, or any other Child of Light has completed a level of growth and is ready to begin a new level, you shall become aware of my temptations. It may only be a thought in your mind. It may come as a feeling of being tired of your involvement and saying to yourself, "perhaps I should give all this up. What am I proving to myself?"

Many times, I work in very subtle ways. I am not trying to deceive you. I am trying to find out who you are, how determined and committed you are. Only in this way can you serve your Father.

It has just been told to me that while I am here perhaps some of you would like to ask me questions. If so, I will answer them for you.

Questions and Answers

Question: Do you work from a pre-planned agenda, from free will, or from both expressions?

Answer: I am part of the Divine Plan. All is always in order.

Question: It is my understanding that you form the other end of the spectrum so that there is duality on Earth. Is this true?

Answer: That was quite beautifully put. I notice how carefully you avoided the use of the word, negative. Instead of calling vibrations positive or negative, let us just call them higher and lower, for that is in true essence exactly what they are. All energy is Light, it all comes from one source. The different degrees of intensity or vibration either elevate it higher or have it at a lower frequency. Let us say that I am responsible to a great extent for the control and dissemination of some of the lower levels of energy. I am also responsible for their dispensation. It also falls to me that they are also not misused, for we are dealing many times at an elemental level, and strict control must be maintained. It is not our function here to cause damage, not at all.

Question: Do you ever not enjoy your work?

Answer: Yes. I do not enjoy my work when I fail. By failing I mean that when I am testing a Child of Light who fails, who falls to temptation and chooses to leave his path for personal gain or greed. In essence it may seem that I win, but in the winning I am sad, for in truth I have lost. In these situations, I am not too happy with some of my work.

Question: I am pleased that you are here at last, for I have known you for over twenty years.

Answer: I have many things to say to you, for indeed you and I have done battle many, many times. The last time, unfortunately, I almost won. I hope you have perspectives and priorities now. I see you slipping into temptations now and then. I could offer you some advice, but I am not allowed to do this for it would be con-tradictory to my purpose. All I can truly say to you is that you know who and where you are and what you are here to do. One day perhaps you shall stop allowing outside vibrations to direct and control your life and shall assume the control of it yourself. Then you and I shall part company. Until that time, I shall be here.

Question: I understand that Hitler was a very high spiritual soul. How long did it take him to fall?

Answer: The soul of the man known as Adolph Hitler was not only highly evolved from a spiritual level but was very talented from an intellectual standpoint. The prime mistake that he made was in falling prey to the temptation to have his Aryan race which, by the way, he himself was not even a member of. This passion is what began his drive to exterminate the Jewish people which immedi-ately sealed his doom. What can I say. He is one of the classic ex-amples of the times I am not happy within what it is I must do, and yet, who is to say? Perhaps what he did was counterbalanced out and may have become a deterrent that might save this planet from another world war.

Question: Did our Father select you for this work? Did you just fall into it? I am curious about this.

Answer: This may sound blasphemous, and I do not recall having ever said this before. I am what is known as the Divine Complement, or the opposite expression of the Spirit of Christ. As He is our Father's Son, so am I. He works through the vibrations of Love. I work through the vibrations of greed. They are the same, only at different extremes. This is the purpose of my creation, the purpose of my work/ and I am as necessary to the continuity and continuation of this world as He is. One without the other cannot survive.

Question: Could you tell us about the Biblical War in the spiritual realms?

Answer: There are many versions of what is known as the Biblical War in Heaven. In actuality there are some who may not even call it a war but a realignment of the balance of energy flows. The most common story is that I, Lucifer, became jealous and took to me my legions to fight our Father for control of the heavens. I lost and was banished to the deepest depths of blackness. This is hogwash. It sounds good, for this way the "evil" one was punished justly, but there is no evil. There are only degrees of love.

At the time that this war was supposed to have occurred what transpired was as follows: There was an imbalance in the expression of vibrations, and it was necessary to transfer some souls from one expression to another. There were many souls unwilling to do this. They rebelled. They were not forced to change or alter their expression; however, there was great pressure placed upon them to do this for their Father.

I will not say to you that there is not most of the time a struggle between different vibrations taking place in the ethers, for there is. There are what you call negative expressions of souls, incarnated souls as well as discarnate souls fighting for control of an area, a planet, a civilization to gain power.

Sometimes for a while the negativity may prevail, but in the long analysis our Father always wins. He holds the edge. He has the unbeatable combination, the Energies of Divine Love. We know that even in this turmoil there is growth, for there is always understanding when the turmoil has subsided.

You must begin to not look at a situation for the moment it occurs. You are all evolved enough in your growth to begin to look at your existence in a broader scope, and not handle a situation for that situation but to look at it in a broader perspective, on a larger scale. You must understand that one situation is relatively unimportant and has no long-range meaning. It is the overall total picture that you are trying to achieve those matter, not the isolated incident. It matters not who wins the skirmish, it is who wins the war.

Question: It is my understanding that the planet Earth is to become totally evolved into the vibrations of the Christ Love. Is this possible?

Answer: This is possible and shall come to pass, but it shall not occur for quite a while. It is true that the vibrations of this planet are rising now, and this increase shall be in effect by the year 1985. The total overall completion of this energy alteration is still far off. In other words, it is not necessary for your expression to be there to balance the other. Let me put it this way: as long as the awareness of both ends of the scale is present the expression can be at either end. Once one disavows the existence of either end of the vibrationary scale then they are in trouble, for they are open to attack, so to speak, for they have released their protection. It is as if I were to say to someone who has passed their last level of initiation, "Well, you have now graduated school, and no one will bother you anymore." That would sound nice; however, the truth and reality is that it does not matter how highly evolved you are. Your testing goes on for as long as you are in physical form. The tests of dedication, discernment in all areas never cease. You are always reminded who you are and what awaits you when you relax and forget who you are. That is the point, to always remember who you are.

Question: You, of all souls, have perhaps had the most difficult path in that you have had to constantly maintain the balance between the extremely high and low vibrations. Can you give us any guidelines as to how to maintain this balance?

Answer: I would not like to deny you an answer, but if I give you the answer then I am worthless to you, so let me say this. If you will allow yourself to be affected by the vibrations that surround you within your society, within your political and economic structure then you shall succumb to the vibrations of the masses, and you shall never achieve that balance. If you will concentrate instead on increasing your own flow of energies, indeed you shall not be affected, for you shall not recognize the existence of, nor allow those other energies to enter into your life. Then you can achieve and maintain your balance. It sounds a lot simpler than it is, for you have to put up with me every step of the way. Understand that I am a great obstacle in your path when you are trying to find out what your mission is for your Father and cannot figure it out.

You come and ask this poor fellow here what your mission is. He wouldn't tell you any more than I would. That's about the only thing he and I agree on. You are the only one that can create and control the balance of your energies, and it is true that you must overcome the temptations that will consistently try to draw you out of your balance.

Now, the purpose is not to draw you out of your balance. The purpose is to strengthen your will and your mind so that you can maintain the balance. If, however, you are weak enough to succumb then there is an alternate for the place you have just left.

If this sounds cold and callous, I am sorry. It is not intended to be that way, but you understand that the work will be done one way or the other. It is our intention to build you, not destroy you. The harder you fight against temptation, the stronger becomes your convictions, the more indestructible becomes your determination. That is what we are all trying to achieve.

Now it is time for me to go. We shall return another time. I must say that I have truly enjoyed this interchange, and perhaps our Father shall ask me to return again. Do not concern yourselves with "catching" my vibrations. I shall leave you all clean and pure.

Goodnight.

Chapter 13

Good evening and Bless you. This is Toran speaking.

At this time, I am going to introduce to you another soul who has not shared with you before, but whose energies have been requested to be shared with you this night. The purpose is twofold, primarily to share the information he has brought with him, and also to allow for the linkage of vibrations, for he shall be speaking at the channeling this Saturday night also. So, we shall take your leave for a few moments.

Kryon: Earth Settlement 125,000 Years ago.

My name is Kryon, and I Bless you.

In your language my name would be spelled Kryon. My energies come to you from the Universe known as Quadrille 5, a long, long distance away. It is my purpose and function on this occasion to describe for you a civilization that I was involved with on your planet approximately one hundred and twenty-seven thousand years ago.

It was, in essence, an experimental group numbering no more than thirty thousand beings. We were transported here magnetically and, shall we say, reassembled on this planet. Our physical structures were different in many aspects than yours. Due to the purpose and nature of our incarnation here we required added protective measures such as body covering, what you refer to as skin of extremely thick texture covered with hair for protection and warmth. We possessed great physical strength, both male and female. We had with us at the conscious level all of our development and abilities in uses with energies and other types of manifestations.

We were approximately your height, perhaps stockier than the average man. We settled in an area in South America in the mountains of what is now Peru. Our function was to establish and set up scientific stations for monitoring of vibrations on this planet. This was to be done to help determine and ascertain the level of soul vibrations to properly inhabit this planet in the future.

We brought with us the abilities of dematerialization, and in this manner from our central base point we were able to survey and travel to most areas of this planet. Part of our function was to locate specific areas for the future construction of energy beacons known to you as pyramids. They were to be used as points of entry, as energy transfer and relay stations from energies traveling to and from space to the center of the Earth.

Much of the information that we compiled relating to the location of the energy beacons was, shall we say, suspended in energy form in the ethers above this planet. This was done so that when the time became proper for the information to be released to those who were to construct these pyramids, the energies, locations, size, and shapes were there to be drawn upon and utilized properly. There are pyramids on this planet that are larger than the one known as the "Great Pyramid" in Egypt.

There are several active pyramids in this State of Arizona that you live in. They are buried in the sands south of the city of Tucson.

This civilization remained on this planet for almost two thousands of your years. It was a short span of time; however, it was all that was required to complete the task for which we came. When our work was completed here, we left exactly as we came.

We did not exist in only one incarnation during our stay here. We were all aware that upon releasing the physical vehicle we would return almost immediately to continue our work. Each incarnation lasted approximately five hundred of your years.

About one hundred and four thousand years ago another civilization was established around the area of what is known today as Mexico City. This civilization was established according to the recommendations and specifications that we had resolved from habitation on the planet in accordance with the level of vibrations present on the Earth at that time.

To the naked eye perhaps you might call them grotesque, for they were very wooly creatures. They were quite heavy in structure with many layers of fatty tissue beneath their skin for warmth and protection. Understand that this civilization at the soul level was highly advanced and developed, and only assumed this rudimentary form to adapt to incarnation on this planet. One might say that they bore some resemblance in their bodies to your gorilla or apes although there was no direct relationship between the two.

This civilization existed in that area for some forty-seven hundreds of your years. They erected thirty-seven pyramidal structures during their stay to serve various functions. This strata of incarnation was deemed a success, and was used later on as a basic plan of physical structure for what you refer to as the early Neanderthal man.

I must say to you that throughout history there have been many landings and other beings from other planets and worlds walking the surface of the planet Earth. Most of them were for relatively short periods of time. Many of them were here to conduct experiments. Some of the experiments were to compare with other worlds under construction elsewhere in other universes. As you know all is interlocked, all is truly connected and in balance.

Try to picture in your minds the planet Earth as a soft cushiony ball whose surface is pliable allowing it to pulsate, to project in areas and to indent in others. It would give the illusion of being a living organism that may seem to be breathing. As we would stare at it, we would see areas rising, and others being depressed, never in a constant pattern. This is indeed an accurate description of your planet. The rising and the falling are stages of evolution and growth. Change is constant.

In the Fall of this coming year there shall be an undetected landing in the Arizona deserts. This shall be to test and check for vibration evolution and any structured Earth changes that may be in the process of taking place. This shall be done to better acquaint your brothers in space with the cyclic changes that are occurring within the structure of this planet. This will help them to better perform their functions for you.

This concludes the message I have brought for you this evening. I hope that I have given you some insight into the true complexity that is involved in creation and habitation of a planet, for I have truly only scratched the surface this night. We shall meet again, and for now I Bless you in the Creator's Name.

Toran: Energy Alignment

This is Toran. Bless you.

At this time, I would like you all to place yourselves in a position of meditation. It is time for us to begin to prepare your vibrations for the future. I do not believe that I have mentioned my prime function here to you before, but it is to prepare your vibrations and align them with those of your brothers in space so that when the proper time arrives the capability for communication and energy transportation aboard ship will be there. We shall begin this preparation now.

The energy shall come to you through your Third Eye and shall last for several minutes you may rest now.

Kryon mentioned to you that his Universe was called Quadrille 5, and I shall explain to you what this refers to. The energies throughout Creation travel and run through patterns of grids almost resembling what you would refer to as graph paper, the flows balancing and counterbalancing each other, keeping the energy system in Creation in harmony and balance at all times. It is these grids of energy that are utilized for magnetic transportation from one area to another. The grids are divided into specific and exact sectors. Some of these sectors are called Quadrilles, some of them are called Quasars, some are called Lighterns.

The system of grids enables communication and transportation involving unbelievable distances in a matter of moments. The grid system is also utilized by ships to transport them rapidly from one area to another. It is in relation to these energy grids that the beacon pyramids were constructed and directed within the concentration of their energy flows to enable them to have linkage and connection at critical points within the grids. Also to establish the planet as part of the overall network or pattern.

Now my brethren we are going to return your attention for the balance of the evening to your beloved Moses, for he has much to share with you this night, and we Bless you.

Moses: Law of Vanity

These are the energies of Moses. Bless you.

It will take a few more moments to reacclimate ourselves back to our own universal vibrations. I wish to speak to you this night concerning more of your Father's Laws.

We discuss with you now the "Law of Vanity", of self-adulation. Is it proper for man to cut his hair, to shave off his beard? Is it proper for woman to artificially color her hair, to use cosmetic products on different parts of her body? Is this proper, or is this an expression of ego in the area of vanity?

If we take ourselves back to the biblical days, we find that the ancients left their hair unshorn. Who was man to cast away what God had bestowed upon him? Indeed, for that time that was their truth. If a man were to have his locks shorn, he would have been ostracized, perhaps even stoned. How does this apply today? It does not. There are many areas of orthodoxy in religions throughout the world where the hair is not shorn, where artificial means applied to the body for beauty are forbidden, for this is their truth. But the evolvement of mankind both intellectually and spiritually have brought us to the point where man realizes that these small things do not place one in a position of turning from God, nor do they prove one's devotion to God. So, it has become a matter of free will and taste basically relating to where one is in the position of one's life. Generally speaking, those that are involved deeply within the material, social vibrations are more prone to utilize this cosmetic method of beauty and prolonging of superficial youth. The importance of these things wanes as one moves into elevated spiritual vibrations. Then one understands that the true beauty shows from within.

In some areas of life, we may come to a point of conflict with vanity. Is it vanity, or is it care of self? Is it vain for one to exercise to keep one's physical body trim and firm? The vanity comes into play when we determine the purpose for the course of action. If the accent is overly stressed in the vibrations of vanity whereby one's growth and balance of life suffer, then indeed the individual is in error.

As you will grow you shall find that the aging process becomes of total unimportance to you, that your relationship with this process fades away and you just are and just be. At this point the energies of vanity become suppressed and no longer play a major role in your life.

Moses: The Law of Exchange

We talk to you about the "Law of Exchange". The law states as follows: "If an individual utilizes and exercises the energies of giving to another human being then he must make himself available and open to receive like energies in return." A simple law, and yet perhaps one of the most difficult for mankind to observe properly. Man is brought up from childhood to learn to give, not to "take". That is the key, the word "take". A bad choice of combinations of letters, for there is only giving. The word "take" implies drawing to oneself without permission. If one wishes to return energies to you, to give to you, you are not taking you are receiving. You are allowing others to exercise the same vibrations that you yourself have exercised, and you have no right to deny them this right.

The Law of Exchange falls under the vibrations of the Laws of Prosperity. If one gives and denies a return flow, then he has stopped the flow of his prosperity. Your teachers share with you of their energies and their knowledge, and the young student who does not have the capability of exchanging energies at equal levels may find another method of exchange; a Blessing, a basket of fruit, an exchange of currency, or a passing on of information to others. They give upon receiving so that others may give and give and give to allow more and more to receive.

Create a world of growth where no one takes, just receives the flow of life and love. If you are to assume your role within the spiritual vibrations you must observe the Law of Exchange, for until you do you have restricted your vibrations.

Moses The Law of Self-Denial

The last law we shall discuss this night is the "Law of Self-Denial". The law is stated as follows: "He who judges himself unworthy shall indeed be denied worthiness. He who deems himself worthy shall flow in the mainstream of prosperity." Man is a multi-level being. The conscious mind within its insecurities may decide that one is unworthy of energies that are coming to him. But what is unworthiness? Is it fear? Is it lack- of self-confidence? Is it awe? It is all of them! In essence, it is judgment, judgment of self.

We have spoken to you before in the areas of suffering. You have heard many times that your Father is Divine Love and is incapable of imposing suffering upon you. Therefore, the imposition of suffering is truly your own manifestations.

Denial is the imposition of suffering, to say to yourself that you are unworthy and therefore, you must suffer and do without is self-denial. Who are you unworthy in relation to? There is no one to compare yourself to but you. You are your Temple. You are unto yourself alone. You have no right to deny the flow, the fluidity to the God within you.

Some will say that they deny themselves out of humility. They wish to be humble. They do not wish to give the impression that they are greedy or walking in ego, so they deny themselves. They are judging others' reactions to themselves. For this decision they are indeed walking in ego, for they are placing themselves in a position of ascertaining that they know the reactions of others before it occurs.

Deny yourselves nothing. Receive all that is offered and tendered to you, for it is all yours. Allow it to come to you with open arms, experience it, utilize it, and allow others to receive it from you.

These are the energies I share with you this night. I Bless you in your Father's Name, and I bid you Shalom.

Chapter 14

Question and Answers: Toran, Kryon, Lucifer

This is Toran speaking. Bless you.

Every fourth week of this series shall be a night for questions and answers. All energies who have shared with you during the preceding period shall be available for questions. So, this evening you may ask your questions of myself, Kryon, the energies of Moses and Lucifer. Please direct your question to the proper energies and allow a few moments for the switchover of vibrations from one level to another. You may proceed.

Question to Toran: Has there ever been a civilization incarnated on this planet that has totally followed God's Path, or come close to it?

Answer: May I rephrase your question for you? Are you asking if there has ever been a civilization on this planet that has carried with it the vibrations of completion of their karmic pattern? Is this what you are asking? ("Yes, I think that answers my question.") Incarnations on this planet have not been designed for this type of pattern, for the vibrations of this planet have not yet evolved to the point to carry that level soul in great numbers. Those souls, and there are many who do reach that level here, have generally as a group served much of their pattern elsewhere and are here for service. There are many planets of higher vibrations that would serve in the category of what you call "completion" of patterns of learning.

Question to Kryon: Is there any connection between the settlement of your people in Peru and the Incas?

Answer: There is in fact a strong direct relationship. When the Incas settled on this planet their group as a whole patterned their physical vehicles according to the standards set many thousands of years before their arrival. In that respect there is a strong correlation. If you are asking me if they were direct descendants, the answer would have to be no.

("Where did the Incas come from and what was their purpose here?")

The Incas as a civilization came to Earth from another Light World. The name of the Light World is spelled Purlo. Their function here was indeed to set up communication bases, to begin to spread knowledge and build a foundation for future growth that was to occur on this planet. Their civilization was quite highly evolved, although many of their methods and modes of living may seem to have been primitive by your standards. They were designed for their needs, for that was all that they needed. They played a strong contributing role in establishing vibration patterns on Earth, and also in the erecting of structures to serve as beacons and guidance for ships. Parts of their blood lines have been maintained and still exist at this time.

Once the civilization was established here, they were joined by some of the Elders from Atlantis, and jointly worked together in many areas.

Question to Toran: I would like to know some of the origins and numbers of our space brothers in the southern hemispheres. Are they counterparts of the Jupiter 1 ship?

Answer: Part of the fleet of ships over the area of Australia and Nev; Zealand do belong to the Jupiter fleet. There are fourteen of them in that vicinity. However, there are ships from other fleets in that area. We would suggest that upon your arrival in Australia that you attempt to contact one known as Kerman in your meditations. He is Commander of Jupiter #27, one of the ships in that area. He shall serve you in the areas of guidance and information during your stay there.

Question to Kryon: Can you tell me from what planet the Mayans came?

Answer: The Mayan civilization came to Earth from the Galaxy spelled Carix. Their civilization was here basically on the same type of mission that the Incas came here for. They were more highly evolved in many areas and left more treasures and records of history for man to discover and learn the truths about their civilization at that time. They were constantly involved in space travel. They were often taken aboard ship physically and returned at a later date. This was done to facilitate an exchange of data and information accumulated on the planet. Through many of the transcriptions and translations of their writings one could note the constant reference to the giant "birds" that descended from the sky to lift them to the heavens. Parts of the energies of this civilization also are present here at this time as a result of breeding. The actual civilization ceased to incarnate here when their work was completed.

Question to Kryon: Did the Inca nation also have space communication similar to the Mayans?

Answer: They did. Much of their communication was done at a mental level rather than physically transporting them aboard ship. The degree of the soul evolution of the Incas was of a nature that they were highly developed in this area of mental communication. Part of their inscriptions and writings do carry some of the vibrations and characters of the language from space that will once again be utilized on this planet shortly.

("Is that part of the symbology you were talking about before?")

Yes.

("What signification is the five-pointed star in symbology")

The five-pointed star was used to denote and signify the location of energy quadrants that bisected the pattern of magnetic grids and helped to determine the vortexes throughout the atmosphere of this planet.

Question to Toran: Are there any spaceships in northern Arizona over the area between Flagstaff and Winslow, and what are the vibrations in that area?

Answer: There are ships in the Flagstaff, Winslow area. There are ships present of both extremes of vibrations, positive and negative. This is necessary to maintain the balance in that area. The vibrations in that area are pure and clean and will remain that way for quite some time. The area around Flagstaff shall develop into a spiritual community; however, it shall not be a large factor as a spiritual community. The coolness of the temperature is conducive to growth only to a limited point; beyond that point those who wish to continue their growth shall have to move to a more temperate climate.

Question to Toran: You have indicated that certain geographical areas in the United States and all over the world are being developed as spiritual energy centers. Does each center have a specialized vibration, and if this is so, what is the specialized vibration of Phoenix and Denver?

Answer: The system of spiritual centers that shall exist within each nation is similar to the divisions from Spirit Core. For example, within the boundaries of the United States there shall be twelve Light Centers with the city of Phoenix serving as the core of the energies. So, each center shall be tied to the core in the base vibration. However, their exact energies shall vary to adjust for the expression and function of each center. Each area of the country shall have variations in vibrations, and those residing in each area and center shall have the same variations.

There shall be a strong tie between Phoenix and Denver and its outlying communities. The ties have already been established and shall become stronger as time passes.

("Is Golden, Colorado one of the satellite communities, and what is its purpose?")

It is one of the satellite communities. The purposes of all the centers are basically the same. They shall be a haven for the Children of Light to attend, to awaken and to grow. The only variations shall occur in the methods used to achieve growth, and in the different degrees of vibrations of those attending each center. For example, we shall find children of higher vibrations whose service is of a higher degree becoming one with the vibrations here in Phoenix. Those who work may not require a high evolution and will be drawn to a center elsewhere.

Question to Toran: Will there also be twelve children's centers within the twelve Light centers?

Answer: This is absolutely true. Each center shall have within it satellite divisions. They shall be located in the outlying communities, and will number either seven, nine or twelve. In each area one of the divisions shall encompass a children's "ranch" where the youth of today, and those who shall be serviced tomorrow, shall come to learn God's ways and develop spiritually. Truly it is only in this way that civilization shall rise to the heights of Universal Love.

("Will the ranches not be run by the children themselves?")

Yes, but under adult supervision.

Question to Toran: Could you name the twelve Light Centers in this country?

Answer: Phoenix, Seattle, Denver, Dallas, Baltimore, Atlanta, New Orleans, near Chicago, and the following states where the city has not yet been determined; New Mexico,

Virginia, Minnesota, South Dakota. In those areas where I have only mentioned the state, they shall be the last centers established, for due to the changing of vibration patterns the exact locations may have to be altered.

("Will the Directors of all the centers come from the Phoenix area, or be trained by the Phoenix Center?")

Most of the Directors shall come from the area where the center will be established. However, there shall be correlation and directions from Phoenix in the process of establishing and coordinating all the centers.

("Is there a name given to this network?")

We could create one for you. Suppose we call them the Twelve Temples of Light.

Question for Toran: If you link all the twelve centers together, will they form a triangle?

Answer: The energies of the twelve centers consist of interlocking triangles and pyramids. In this way, and it has been designed as such, we shall have a constant flow and exchange of energies from one triangle to another. This will create an overlapping and support of energies back and forth rather than having a separation of the triangles. It will be a total support system.

Question to Toran: How long will it be before the centers will be established?

Answer: The centers will not be all established until after the year 1985 when the energy patterns have completed their changes. At that time the exact location for all the centers will have been determined. Until that time the variance within the energy patterns will delay this determination, nor will it permit the selection of the proper children who are to run the centers. Those who may have been chosen to play a major role in a center may not prepare themselves properly for the vibrational changes that shall occur and may have to be replaced.

Question to Toran: Will there be the same type of centers in Europe as in the United States, and will they be all connected?

Answer: This is correct. Throughout the nations of Europe, as well as Africa, Asia and other continents, there shall be a network of Temples of Light, each in a geographical location that shall tie them directly to others, and to all the others indirectly. In this way the pattern shall be uniform throughout the world.

Question to Toran: Are the locations of the centers based on grids and vortexes for energy and vibrational control?

Answer: Very specifically so, for without the proper location in relation to the energy grids and vortexes, each area would not contain the proper vibrations to nurture and help them achieve their mission.

("Will each center have a temple, A Solomon's Temple, or just Phoenix?")

Yes and no. Some of the centers will have the energy manifestation of the temple only. The actual physical structure will be at the Phoenix Center.

All of the centers will not have the same type of structure or facility. There will be variances according to the vibrations of each location. Each will be designed to utilize the energies in the area to the fullest extent. Each shall contain a form of pyramid to harness the energy flows. There will also be in addition to classrooms and meditation rooms, rooms specifically designed for contemplation and spiritual inspiration that will allow one to tap into creative energies to further stimulate the flow of knowledge.

("Will there be a crystal room?")

Many of the centers will have a crystal room, for the crystals are a prime conductor of magnetic energy and create great intensities of power.

Question to Toran: If the core in America will be Phoenix, can you tell me if the core in Europe will be Egypt?

Answer: The core shall be in Jerusalem.

("Will there be a Temple of Solomon in Jerusalem?")

The temple in Jerusalem shall not a physical one. It will be an "energy" temple emitting all the energies without having the physical structure. The results shall be the same.

I have been urged to ask you at the insistence of one who has been pacing back and forth here, as to why in the hell he has not been asked any questions.

Question to Lucifer: Is it not true that I know you through the energies of Solomon?

Answer: This is quite true my dear, for part of my function is to supply him with a little "sandpaper" for his energies. He by himself is not harsh enough, so periodically I assist him in his work.

Question to Lucifer: When Judas betrayed Jesus did you have anything to do with that, or was Judas aware of what was happening

at the time? Judas loved Jesus more than any other of the disciples. Was that why he took on this task?

Answer: Who says that Judas betrayed Jesus? Doing God's Work
is not betrayal. I am not responsible for all things that seem to be
negative. Some things you people do by yourselves.

("I guess what I really want to know is, was Judas aware that he
was to do that? ")

Absolutely so, and he was doing the service that he was here to
do. We cannot say that he was punished for his act, for in truth he
was not, no more than I am punished for mine.

Always remember that in every situation there are dual expressions. When you are in a situation and the dual expression has not
manifested itself, do not become complacent, for the action will
not be completed until the balance has been achieved. Remember
this, try to think of an instance where this has not occurred for
you.

Question to Lucifer: Could you elaborate on your last statement?

Answer: In every situation of life, or enlightenment, or joy that
occurs for you, somewhere in the energies of the completion of
that situation there is going to be some degree of negativity present, even if it is only a temporary situation. No one has ever been
involved in any project or reached any goal without having been
exposed to some stumbling blocks along the way. If this were to
occur the reaching of the goal would have little value.

You have a phrase, "having things handed to you on a silver plat-
ter"; therefore, you value it not. This is a good example of what I
am talking about. If you are involved in a situation that is going too
smoothly for you, it is, and somewhere along the path an obstacle

will appear to slow you down and work a little harder. This shall create the value of achievement for you.

Question to Lucifer: Do you test by actions as well as thoughts and words? If people do to excess in some areas, is that testing?

Answer: I shall answer your question for you by giving you an example. If an individual is in an incarnation to learn the lessons of greed, I shall do everything in my power to make him as greedy as possible. This is not a situation to laugh at. Understand that this basically applies in all lessons. The temptation must be overcome. Once a temptation is given in to, it increases during the following lifetime making the lesson more difficult to overcome.

Question to Lucifer: You have tested so many. Who has tested you?

Answer: I could enter into a long dissertation about this, but I would have to say that for every soul I have tested, every soul has tested me. Even I am in a system of exchange of energies. There are not too many who succumb to my vibrations willingly. Most times there is resistance, and that is the way it is supposed to be.

If you are asking what has occurred to bring me to the place I am today, then it is a story of a different matter.

("Yes, I am.")

Let it be said that I am a soul, a son of God who has never had to undergo a physical incarnation or growth within a karmic pattern, for since the beginning of my time I have served in spirit form. My growth, as growth in all spirit, occurred within a love vibration, for how could it be possible for me to express the other end of the spectrum if I do not know what the love vibration is. So, it was necessary for even me to experience all energies.

Understand that all spirit learns in spirit form as well as incarnate form. Since the area of service for our Father is a little different than most souls much of my growth and my understanding of what it is I. am here to do has come to me directly from our Father.

As a point of information, I wish you to know that within the confines of Creation I am not alone. There is a "negative agent" within every Universe in Creation. They are not all called Lucifer, they are called by many other names. All Universes need the balance and the negative expression. In many areas and Universes of extremely high evolvement the expression of negativity is softened to a great degree, for they do not require an "agitated" vibration.

In time this too shall apply within this planet. In the year 1985 there shall begin to be a difference in the heaviness of my vibrations. As the awareness rises, the necessity for sternness lessens. I serve as a reminder for them to remember who they are, and to help them keep their feet on the ground. Who knows, one day I might even grow wings.

Every word I speak, every action I take is for a positive purpose, or a negative one. When I make jest, it is done with a purpose, it is done to eliminate fear within you in what you have been taught that I represent. I do not wish to have you fear me. To acknowledge my presence, my role, and what I stand for is what I wish you to understand. I am as necessary a function as all of your spiritual masters and teachers, for this is in truth what I am. I have come to you here to make a beginning, to have a nucleus of Children understand the role I play so that there shall be a beginning somewhere, and perhaps it will spread and eliminate the fear, for the fear is no longer necessary, just the understanding.

Question to Lucifer: I wish to congratulate you, with reluctance, for your efficiency.

Answer: Your congratulations are refused, for they were given in reluctance, not with love.

Question to Lucifer: Is this the first time you have come to a group in this sort of capacity?

Answer: I have on one other occasion spoken in a similar fashion to another group. However, the fear that was created, the fear that the channel endured caused me not to attempt it again for a prolonged period of time until I met this one here and was asked by our Father to do so. He was correct, for he, as well as yourselves, have the strength in your vibrations to accept my energies knowing that you walk in the Light and have nothing to fear. You now have the capacity to share this experience with others which is the purpose for it all.

Question to Lucifer: Is there any difference in the law for your lieutenants and those of the Children of Light?

Answer: Essentially not, they must all understand that they are in service for the Father. As long as they understand this their energies and their work are kept in the proper perspective. This is also true for those who walk with the Children of Light. It is not for their ego, not for their adoration or their pocketbooks, it is for their Father. We are dealing with a lesson against ego and power at both ends of the spectrum.

Question to Lucifer: I would like to Bless you and thank you for coming to us and sharing with us to help us understand so that we can pass it on to others. I truly Bless you for that.

Answer: In our Father's Truth we truly Bless all of you, each and every one, for we have observed you all in your growth. We have been with you all, and shall continue to be with you all, hoping to build you in strength, not tear you down and destroy you. Only in this way shall you be able to face the obstacles and overcome them that lie ahead in your work.

One cannot build a steel wall from putty. It can only be built out of steel, and the steel must be hammered and hammered until it is strong and true and will not bend. So, you must suffer to a degree and endure, but in the end the back will be straight, and the heart as strong as steel, and yet full of love and compassion. Then you shall be able to do your work for your Father.

Now I have chatted enough, and I take your leave and Bless you one and all.

This is Toran.

Before we end tonight's session, we ask you to read portions of your Bible and find an area that involves a negative expression. Read into the negativity and find the function of those energies. Try to ascertain what positive result was or should have been achieved by the imposition of this negativity. For in every situation that occurs to you in your life, when you become aware of the negativity, it is time to pause and seek the reason for the negativity. What positive purpose is it trying to achieve for you, then it shall become known to you, and you shall be able to transmute it to growth and learning energies. This is another lesson in creating your own causes rather than standing still and being effected.

We Bless you, and we end tonight's class at this time with the Love of our Divine Father.

Shalom.

Chapter 15

The Divine Father: Creation of a Universe.

These are the energies of Moses, and I Bless you.

For the first time our circle numbers eighteen, the symbol of the completion of energies. Perhaps this is fitting on this night due to the nature of the class that has been prepared for you. I shall talk to you a little later on in relation to describing more of our Father's Laws pertaining to Creation, and to incarnation and existence on this planet. Before I begin your Father wishes to share a few words with you.

The Father: Creation of a Universe.

Bless you, My Children. This is your Father speaking.

I speak to you tonight through the energies of Michael to allow Us to have a little more force in Our expression to you this night. I am your Father, and in the beginning, it fell to Me, upon the wishes of My Father, Our Creator, to create this Universe you inhabit in both spiritual and incarnate form.

The creation of a Universe is indeed a vastly complex system of multiplying of energies, of patterns of interlocking reactions, taking long, long periods of your time. The discussion this night was opened by Moses, and I truly could speak to you Myself, but the purpose is to undergo a buildup of energies and vibrations so that he will be able to handle the energies that are coming to him now, so be patient for a moment please.

This is your Divine Father My beloved Children, and I Bless you.

Please send him energy as this transmission is most difficult for him. This is the second time I have spoken to you in this manner. I have elected to share with you this night to describe for you the process by which a Universe is created so that you may understand some of the ramifications involved leading to the creation, evolvement and fulfillment of galaxies and solar systems and planets within a specific Universe.

When a soul has reached a point in its evolution where it has, in fact, become Divine Truth, when the properties and qualities of its energies are as One with Mine, it is assigned one final task before total assimilation occurs. This task is the creation of a Universe, to serve in the capacity of a God, a Creator, to assume the responsibility for the development and evolution of countless millions of souls, to teach them His perspective of Divine Love. It is an opportunity for Him to put into action all that He has learned throughout the eons of His Existence since the first day of His creation.

When your Father, the Creator of your Universe whom you refer to as Michael, Sananda and the Spirit was assigned the task of creating your Universe, He went through the following procedure: a pattern of energy grids was established. Each interlocking point and crossover point of energy specifically was located in an exact place. This process was comparable to planting seeds in a field.

Within the limitations of space assigned for this Universe the energies for the basic number of galaxies were set into place, and within the galaxies, the solar systems and the planets. There are at all times additional galaxies coming to life in your Universe, and some dissipating and ending their existence. When these energy seeds were in their proper place, they began to multiply, to grow, much as a soul grows and develops from a single energy cell. When the energy mass has reached the desired proportions for the planet, or asteroid, or star, the process which takes untold millions of your years, the energy is converted into matter. (This processes We shall not describe to you at this time.) A physical, living object has been created. This transmutation involves the releasing of great amounts of heat and energy. Many times, in the creation of a planet it is seen as a ball of flames or light.

When this transmutation has been completed the basic foundation for the beginning planets within the structures of the new Universe have come into existence in their proper locations in their proper areas, and with their proper dimensions. At this point the work just begins, for though We have taken Our Energy and converted it into living matter, We must breathe further life into the planets. We must add to each planet qualities and textures of energies and vibrations specifically designed to bring to each planet the properties and qualities to help it serve in its function for the overall evolution of the Universe.

This is accomplished through the magnetic grid system. Energies are transported through the grids, released through the vortexes in the atmospheres, and allowed to saturate in layers of energy around a planet. They feed their particular qualities to that planet to allow it to assume the proper qualities and structures of energy necessary for its function.

The final development of this story you are already aware of, so I shall not take the time to repeat it to you once again. I have chosen to relate this story to you Myself, and I have done so for one specific purpose so you shall feel My Vibrations, and in the feeling of My Vibrations you will know that the Words I have spoken to you are Divine Truth. What I have said to you is the way it is, for within this lesson there is no room for doubt. All is as I have related it to you.

I take your leave now, My Beloved Children, and I Bless you with Eternal Energy, and look forward to the day in your evolution when We shall again become as One. Bless you one and all.

Moses: The Law of Incarnation

This is Moses my brothers and sisters. Bless you.

Some of the things that have been discussed here over the past several weeks may not have seemed to be properly involved in our study of the Bible, and yet, for our purposes our study of the Bible is the study of Creation. We do not wish to approach this topic and area of knowledge in any type of limited perspective. We wish to be all- encompassing, and to give you as broad a perspective as possible so that your understanding may be complete.

You have experienced something this night that few people share, and for it you are truly Blessed. Treasure the energies that have come to you this night, for their vibrations shall be with you always.

We talk to you tonight about an additional number of our Father's Laws. We begin with a few laws relating to incarnation. The Law states as follows: "When a soul is created, its book of records is established, and a total pattern of learning and growth is established for the soul." This pattern must be completed. The time span for the completion of the pattern is not firmly fixed but is quite flexible. The soul has the freedom to accelerate its levels of growth, and in some cases to muddle through and underachieve. However, the soul is only permitted a clearly defined limited time between incarnations. The law states that as the soul grows within its evolvement, the degree of time that may elapse between incarnations increases. This means that if one has only three or four incarnations left in their pattern, they may elect not to incarnate for many, many hundreds of years. During the earlier and middle levels of growth the soul must assume incarnations within a specific area of time.

Another law states: "A soul may not elect to serve a solitary incarnation on a planet unless that incarnation is one of service for his Father." Within each planet there exists a vibration and pattern of length of incarnations.

For example, when a soul begins its first incarnation on the planet Earth, it signs a "contract", so to speak, from forty-eight to seventy-two incarnations, all told. The leeway is there to allow for rapid growth and evolution. This is done to keep harmony within the vibrations of the planet and the societies as well.

A soul may not voluntarily incarnate in a civilization of a lower vibration. The only exception being if one is acting in the capacity of doing service for the Father to serve as a conscious master or teacher for the purpose of helping to raise and elevate vibrations on a specific planet. Then one acts in the capacity of what we know as an alien soul. In the normal course of evolution, the soul is not permitted to downgrade an incarnation, for it would upset the balance and equilibrium of itself and those living on the planet.

If I go back and look at my life and ask you to take your minds back to the time when our Father first came to me, and I told you that I was frightened and felt unworthy and had no tongue to speak. Many of you said, "how could this be? Here was a man who was a tower of strength, and yet he relied on his brother to do his work for him." You see, my brothers and sisters, it was not a question of weakness or strength, it was a question of sensitivity of vibrations. It was a lack of compatibility on my part with the vibrations around me that caused these feelings of inadequacy and insecurity within me. Of course, at the time I was not aware of this.

Most of you in this room have endured this very thing I speak of. Blessedly you are aware, and so you may overcome this. One of the greatest problems that exists is the acclimation of a highly evolved soul incarnating in a lower vibration to do service, for there is a variable factor involved; it is the strength and determination of the conscious mind. Many people say, "how could our Father allow a child of His to go insane, knowing that the soul was too sensitive to incarnate on this plane?" It has nothing to do with the soul. It has to do with the variable factor, with the conscious being, the choice, the environment under which the child was raised during its formative years which gave it strength or weakness.

Another law: "If an alien soul involved in a service incarnation in a lower vibration is incapable of completing that incarnation, and leaves by any one of a number of methods such as suicide, insanity, or any other abnormal type of departure, the soul is relieved of its responsibility for the service pattern and is allowed to return to the area it came from before the service began."

The reason for this is quite simple. No one wishes to punish a soul, nor is it desired to damage the vibrations of a soul. Once this has occurred it would be necessary for the soul to have extensive re-training before it could successfully re-enter those vibrations, and time does not permit this.

At this point I would like to ask if I have raised any questions or comments in your minds. If I have, we shall take a few moments to answer them for you.

Question: If a soul is in the early to middle stages of its growth, what is the typical number of years between its incarnations?

Answer: The average span between incarnations is approximately forty to sixty of your years. There are exceptions, however. If an incarnation is ended abruptly without warning and planning where the soul has not had the required years necessary to help it fulfill its purpose, it may assume an incarnation as rapidly as two or three of your years. But, as a general rule, it is forty to sixty years.

Question: If a soul does not complete its requirements by the end of its cycle of incarnations, then what happens?

Answer: I am happy to say to you that it has never occurred. There are many souls who become disgruntled, dismayed and disenchanted with their patterns of growth, and do not desire to go on any further. What do they do? Basically, they destroy themselves. They cease to exist by allowing their energies to dissipate without recharging themselves. If we have a soul that is close to the end of its pattern of incarnations, it comes to a point where it no longer has a choice of which lessons it elects to learn. There are not that many left, and so it will assume the balance of its lessons whether it wishes to or not, for that is all that is left for it to accomplish.

Most of all, you must understand that when a soul reaches close to that point in its evolution, it has already begun to be aware of its true identity. Being so close to the completion of its pattern, it would have no reason to refuse to complete its growth. If this situation did occur where for some reason a soul decided it did not wish to complete

its pattern, it would in spite of itself, for this is Divine Law, and it is always in perfect order.

Question: Does the soul have to fulfill its pattern of requirements on only one planet, or can it incarnate on other planets of similar vibrations also?

Answer: Within each specific series of incarnations, they are served on one planet. Understand that each soul, between the beginning and the end, has assumed thousands of incarnations all in set series and different stages of evolution. Each series is undertaken in different galaxies, different solar systems, and different planets, for at each level of growth the quality and level of vibrations is increased, allowing for more advanced growth.

Question: If this is the case, how is it determined which is a soul's "home" planet?

Answer: What we generally refer to as the soul's "home" planet would be the one it left to come to the one where it is currently incarnating on. The "home" planet changes, for if a soul were to complete its series of incarnations here on Earth, and then incarnate somewhere else, it would refer to Earth as its "home" planet. The only true home the soul has is within the vibrations of the Core of Spirit from its creation. The balance is transitory.

Question: If a soul comes to this planet and ends an incarnation early, is it always its choice to go back to the planet it came from?

Answer: It is always their choice, for they have volunteered for the service in the first place. Therefore, it is their choice. It is no different than the karma involved for suicide, for our Father does not punish one for that either. The soul upon reassuming spirit form becomes aware of what it has done and assesses its own lesson, the lesson necessary to correct the variation in its vibrations. The soul at the spirit level knows that its evolution cannot progress as long as there is a "chink" in its vibrations.

Many times, we wonder why we take upon ourselves a severe lesson to learn. We ask ourselves how we could have done this but there truly is no choice. At some point in the pattern of growth it must be resolved.

Question: You said that a soul has anywhere from forty-eight to seventy-two incarnations on the planet Earth at its present level of vibrations. When the level of vibrations has changed on Earth will this remain the same, or change?

Answer: Those souls currently involved in their patterns will finish them. Those beginning their series shall have the series shortened due to the increased vibrations. The new series will be from thirty-six to forty-two incarnations. The longer span will not be necessary.

We would like to resume now to discuss a few more laws before the session ends for this night.

Moses: The Law of Personality

We talk to you about the "Law of Personality". What role does the soul play in relation to the conscious personality? The law states that the soul may in no manner use force or coercion to try to influence the conscious mind in any manner or action. It is the soul's function and responsibility to make the conscious personality aware, aware of its presence, aware of its lessons and its mission. This process begins at the first day of birth and continues during the course of the lifetime, mostly at the unconscious level by the implantation of thoughts, reactions and emotions. It guides the conscious personality toward the desired results, feelings and successes that the soul wishes to achieve during the lifetime.

The soul tries to make the individual aware, not by fear or by threats. This would be a karmic situation for the soul as it would be interfering with the free expression of the personality. However, this is done at times, and there are many who are walking the physical plane who seem to be possessed spiritually, who are not possessed. Their own souls are coercing and forcing them into situations in which they do not wish to be involved. For this the soul shall draw a heavy lesson to itself. The union between the conscious personality and the soul must be accomplished in a love vibration.

One may ask, "what if the conscious personality refuses to accept the presence of the soul? What if it knows that the soul is there and says, go away, don't bother me, I wish to have fun and to play." Is the soul held responsible for the lack of growth in this case? The answer is yes, for somewhere along the way the soul has neglected to do something it should have done. Somewhere it has not been successful in projecting its love and its understanding to the conscious mind. We know, all of us, that the most powerful tool we have is love. If it does not work, and one does not react positively to it, then it has been improperly applied.

When an individual will go through an incarnation without achieving too much growth at the conscious level, we find ourselves involved in another instance where the soul will assume another incarnation in only a few years. Lack of growth in an incarnation is not a desirable result, and it will be strongly suggested to the soul that it enter the physical plane quickly to achieve what it failed to achieve before. It can, in essence, refuse to do this, but that does not occur.

Moses: The Law of Hate

The last law we shall discuss with you this night pertains to the "Law of Hate". It may seem strange to you that your Father would have a law pertaining to hate, for it is a vibration that is not recognized as being in existence. Yet it is a vibration that is expressed by man and must be dealt with properly.

The law states: "When man invokes the emotions and vibrations of total rejection of another human being, or hatred, he shall in his next incarnation be denied the vibrations of love."

These vibrations shall not be denied to him for the total incarnation but until the time comes when he realizes the value of the love vibrations and works and earns the right to receive it once again. The vibrations of hate are those of judgment, almost total judgment. They are also the vibrations of prolonged anger, resentment, and other undesirable qualities. So, it draws a most severe lesson in return. There are many instances throughout history that are recorded in the vibrations of hate, recorded in heinous acts of violence and crimes against humanity as expressions of this hatred.

Let us look at our brother Adolph Hitler, and his hatred for the Hebrew people, a hatred so true that he lost all sense of reason and perspective of life, and then transferred it to millions of Catholics in his search for "purity", his Aryan race.

The vibrations of hatred are the vibrations of total rejection. It is closing the door on another human being, refusing to attempt to understand their truth. The line is very fine. How much difference is there between acceptance and rejection? Perhaps the only difference is in our confidence relating to ourselves that either gives us or denies us the capacity to accept others in their truth.

Now we shall draw tonight's session to a close. We have enjoyed sharing with you once again, and we wish you health and well-being until our next session. We Bless you in our Father's Name. Shalom.

Chapter 16

Toran: The book of Leviticus

This is Toran speaking. Bless you.

Our discussion this night is going to be guided along more of a philosophical nature than it has been for the past several weeks. We are going to discuss man's responsibility to man.

The Book of Leviticus is basically composed of laws that were given to our Brother, Moses, by our Father to apply to the Hebrew people to assist in controlling their behavior, and establish a pattern for their society, as well as for a system of law and order. The prime function of many of these laws was to make man aware of his responsibility to his fellow man. Most of these laws, and the punishments for violation of these laws are quite outdated in today's societies. However, for the time when they applied, they were proper and effective.

We must understand that societies in ancient days were not as organized, as structured, and as controlled as they are today. Each man and his family were a government to themselves. They were responsible for their actions to themselves. There was not the interdependence, one to the other for a standard of living, or for sustenance of life. Each man cared for his own needs.

One basic principle of these laws stated that when a man or a woman violated one of God's Laws, even though they were ignorant of the existence of the law, they were guilty and had to be punished for the violation. This law is in sharp contrast to your beliefs, and the way you guide your lives at this time. We know now that one is not punished for taking an action that one has been ignorant of, but for those times it was necessary for this to be. There had to be examples made to teach others the proper way of life, to help others ascertain what was right and wrong in our Father's Eyes. It is true that many suffered unjustly, for they erred not out of a knowledgeable error, but out of ignorance.

The penance for most crimes, perhaps crimes is not a proper word, let us use the word errors, was basically the same. It involved the sacrifice of a lamb or other animal at the alter to our Father. The repentance for the error was placed into the animal by the individual placing their hands on the head of the animal, atoning for their sins, allowing the sins to flow into the animal, and then sacrificing the animal to our Father as a symbol of penance and atonement.

To ask for atonement or forgiveness today in this manner would bring down the wrath of many who work for the better treatment of animals, etc. But, of course, we must relate the method of atonement to the times and the conditions that prevail. It was indeed our Father's Request that atonement be performed in this manner at that time, and so it was.

Relationships between men and women existed under a system of laws that were quite specific. Sexual limitations were not stringent, but they were clearly defined relating to sexual activities within a family structure. They forbid sexual relationships within bloodlines, relatives by marriage, and intercourse involving animals. It was written that if this occurred, the animal and the human both were to be slain. In spite of the establishment of these laws there were many occasions throughout history where cities were established that became dens of iniquity, places where carnal behavior went rampant. Eventually whole cities had to be destroyed. An example of this was the city of Pompei.

Let us examine the philosophy relating to the violation of a law in ancient biblical days in relation to the violation of a law at this time. By doing this you shall be able to see the comparative evolution and gaining of responsibility for the soul of its actions. We are aware at this time that our Father is not a punishing, threatening God. We know that He is Love, and that when we err, we ourselves establish the corrective lesson and the situation to work out the error. We know that this must be done in order for us to continue our growth and development.

If we look at the Scriptures it is written that our Father judged that He set the laws, and the rules, and the standards, and the punishments for the errors or sins as they were referred to at that time. The individual was not allowed the freedom of choice within this area. If the set of laws that applied in ancient biblical days were still in force at this time there would be much discontent, for the soul today knows its responsibility. It has evolved to the point where it accepts the responsibility for its actions,

and to correct its errors. So, mankind is allowed a wider range of choice and course of action, many times even encouraged to take a course of action that may seem to be detrimental to his growth in the long run, if it will assist him in learning a lesson.

Control over the incarnated soul was far more rigid than it is today. You could compare it to a parent being stricter with a child in its tender years than one who is in its teens. As the child matures it becomes more responsible for its actions. Such is the case with all of mankind.

The average man in those days knew not of the "Laws of Cause and Effect". They felt that all was caused by our Father. Today mankind is encouraged to establish his own truth, to create his own causes. This system could not have worked in ancient days, for they were not capable of handling those types and levels of energies.

The basic vibration under which a spiritual law is initiated and put forth always remains constant. If not, all would not always be in Divine Order. It is the progression and the interpretation of the law that alters and expands as the level of soul evolvement increases. With each expansion of the vibrations of a law, the soul is allowed more and more freedom of expression, for it becomes more and more responsible and aware of its actions.

I wish to take a few moments to speak to you in another area. I wish to remind you that I have said to you the first time I spoke to you that my prime function here is to prepare your vibrations for either contact or communication with your brothers and sisters in space. I have been in and within most of your vibrations to this point. Many of you have on occasion, been feeling poorly, experiencing various types of muscle pain, soreness, inflammation, excessive tiredness, the flu and other types of cleansings. I have not caused these things to happen to you, and yet they are a result of my presence here. As your vibrations are being prepared to receive higher energies and compatibility with these energies, there are always adjusting reactions taking place in your bodies. The most important thing I wish you to be aware of is the tiredness that you shall feel. To overcome this we suggest that you, in your meditations, ask to have your energies transported to Jupiter 1 for healing and re I do not wish you to dwell upon the thought that you may be taking a journey into space. I want you to hear my words and file them away. Then continue your life as it flows for you, not to waste a moment's energy on something that is not a reality for you at this time. I know and understand that it is impossible for you to accept and believe when I say to you that you may be physically taken aboard ship. So, I do not ask you to do this, just to be aware that the possibility may exist for you to do so.

Now I turn the balance of this program for tonight over to our brother Moses, and I take your leave and Bless you.

Moses: The Law of Food and Diet

These are the energies of Moses, and I Bless you.

When our Father was handing down the laws pertaining to the existence of His children, one of the categories of law pertained to food and diet. I would like to discuss them with you and enlighten you in this area, perhaps creating a better understanding as to the purpose for these laws.

The laws were basically designed for health. The prime law relating to meat was stated thusly: "Meat may be eaten from an animal that has a hoof split all the way up and chews its cud." The cud symbolizing the cleansing of the food that the animal eats itself. For this reason, the Hebrews were not allowed to eat meat from a pig, for although it has a cloven hoof, it has no cud to chew. What was not stated in the law was the fact that the meat from this animal was, at that time, quite difficult to preserve as it spoiled and became tainted quite rapidly. Man was forbidden to eat the flesh of the vulture, the owl, the hawk, the eagle, the raven, for these were themselves birds of prey and were unclean.

The same law applied to fish. Man was permitted to only eat fish that had scales on its skin. Those members of the sea world with hard shells were essentially scavengers, and therefore unclean. It seems rather strange that our Father would take the time and effort and find it important to issue laws relating to man's diet. It would seem that sooner or later man would figure it out for himself as he would find the incompatibility with certain types of foods. However, you must understand that at the time the laws were handed down the Hebrews were as lost children having no home, having wandered for many moons. They were open to temptation, to error and to being easily swayed, so it was necessary to spell out for them a daily course of conduct for their lives, as a mother would do for a child.

The laws relating to diet have changed to a degree. Traditionalists still observe them to the letter, but modern methods of food preparation and preservation have eliminated the necessity for many of the ancient laws pertaining to health. Yet, when individuals evolve beyond a certain point in their growth, they find themselves developing an incompatibility with those categories of food specifically forbidden in the ancient days. In essence, they return to the observance of the ancient laws, and the cycle runs full.

Let us go back to perhaps our first or second class when we spoke of the Garden of Eden, when we spoke of what Adam and Eve sustained themselves with: nuts, berries, and fruits, and were pure of heart and spirit. Will not the time come again when the Garden of Eden shall return, and man once more shall have as his diet fruits, nuts, and berries? Indeed, it shall, for his vibrations will have risen to the level where ingestion of lower vibrations of food will not be possible, and another cycle shall have run its course.

Moses: The Law of Spiritual Union

We talk to you now of another of God's Laws. We speak of the "Law of Spiritual Union". The law states, "When a relationship between two souls has been established by the blending and union of spiritual vibrations, the relationship shall be Blessed by our Father and shall perpetuate itself."

What does this mean to the average man? What it means is this: When two are involved in a relationship and have as a foundation and basic principle of this relationship a spiritual union of vibrations, this relationship shall be Blessed by their Father and shall endure, never dissipate, and always remain constant and fulfilling. When two people shall enter into a relationship based on conscious emotional involvement, whether it be sexual, or expressed in other physical areas, it shall be entered into because of the lessons involved between the two souls. If within this relationship a spiritual relationship does not occur, the relationship shall dissipate and eventually end.

This is why we say to you that a marriage is a union of vibrations, not of emotions. Why is it that so many men and women that are married seek elsewhere for fulfillment for themselves? They do this for they have placed themselves in a limiting situation that does not allow them the fulfillment that they need at all levels of their existence. They have entered the relationship without a solid foundation and reasoning.

I do not mean to infer that there is only one person with whom you can establish a spiritual union, for this is not true. There are many with whom a spiritual compatibility is possible. The key is the awareness and the sensitivity to recognize this compatibility when it appears to you; then you shall have a relationship without frustrations, jealousies, and angers. It will be one of trust and harmony and love, for the knowledge will be there that the vibrations shall not change but shall be constant.

We talk to you about the law pertaining to the responsibility to offspring. Where does parents' responsibility to their offspring begin, and where does it end? If it is true that man's prime responsibility is to self, then how can we justify so much self-sacrifice for their children, not only during their formative years, but as many carry it with them for the balance of their lives. In the ancient biblical days when a boy reached the age of thirteen years, he was considered a man, and was set free to be responsible for himself and for his actions, always to be respective to his parents but to pursue his life and be responsible for it.

Today, children, upon reaching the age of thirteen, are far more mature and wiser than their counterparts in ancient days. Yet, in many cases, they are tightly controlled and held down by parental authority. The key to the proper attitude is to understand that your child is a person, an individual who is with you for a while, and upon maturity assumes the responsibility for his own life and actions. At that moment the essence of the parents' responsibility has ended, and they begin to serve in the capacity of a friend and advisor. Many parents hold on too tightly during the formative years, and it becomes too difficult to release at the proper time, so both suffer, the parent and the child. It becomes increasingly more important with each generation for the parent to understand its role in relation to the child, for the children are coming in more and more aware, and need the freedom of expression to enable them to remain open spiritually.

Moses: The Law of Personal Morality

We speak to you of the "Law of Personal Morality". The law states as follows: "An individual must set standards for his moral behavior in accordance with his own truth. If, however, his truth is diametrically opposed to the laws set down by the society in which he is living, he must either adjust his moral behavior, or relocate himself to a society that is compatible with his beliefs."

No man has the right to set moral standards for another, for no man walks in another man's truth. When you have established a moral code for yourself, and you violate it, you draw a lesson to yourself. You have, of course, imposed it upon yourself, for you have set your truth and violated it, and must take the responsibility for your actions. What are you supposed to do if within your truth you desire to take an action that others do not believe to be proper? The answer is quite clearly defined. If in taking this action others will consciously suffer, and you are aware of this, you shall draw a lesson to yourself if you take the action. If you take the action in such a manner so that others do not suffer as a result of the action, then it is proper for you to do so, for it is your truth.

The line becomes quite fine at times, and yet it is there. No one is intended to ever be denied the expression of their truth, but the circumstances and conditions must be proper for its expression.

Moses: "Law of Man's Responsibility to His Ego"

We shall discuss one more law with you this night, the "Law of Man's Responsibility to His Ego". This may sound like a strange law, but it is a reality, for ego is a reality. Perhaps we should begin by giving you our definition of ego.

Ego is an emotional reaction or response based on a previous experience within a given situation or circumstance. What is man's responsibility to his ego? Is man to totally suppress his ego? By no means, for by doing so he puts a chain around the expression of his conscious personality, he eliminates the factor necessary to motivate him and assist him toward successfully achieving his goals. The expression of ego is valid, for it exists. The key is along what point along the scale of its expression is he within a safety factor? The answer is when man will utilize ego as a tool for growth and expression, it is proper. When the ego utilizes man to achieve its end, he is involved in an improper situation.

Many times, I am saddened when I see one who has grown spiritually and has achieved a certain amount of success and fame and allows his ego to break free and take control and move the life out of perspective. Many times, this will cause a child to be lost to his Father. It is for this reason that many times doubts are placed in your mind, doubts as to the validity of your truth, your spiritual communication, to force you to keep your ego in perspective,

to remind you that you are not perfect. Do not try to hide your pleasures and emotions, express them, and enjoy them, for many times they are a return of energy for much effort and energy expended. However, know that the time for elation and back-slapping has a limit, and when its expression is over your work must continue.

Next week we are going to begin to relate to you the spiritual symbology involved within some of the characters of the ancient Hebrew alphabet and the language of hieroglyphics, for in these languages are many of the keys of Creation.

Now it is time for us to end our lecture for this evening. We take your leave and Bless you in our Father's Name.

Shalom.

Books by Dr. Frank Alper

Exploring Atlantis Vol. 1, Vol.2, Vol. 3 combined (from 1981 – 1986) ISBN 978-1-4475-4994-9

Our Existence is Mind, Healing Methods for the 3rd Millenium. ISBN 978-3-9524451-2-9

A series of spiritual lectures channeled through the Soul of Rev. Frank Alper D.D.:

Moses and the Bible Vol. 1 (1980) ISBN 978-3-9524930-8-3

Moses and the Bible Vol. 2 (1980) ISBN 978-3-9524930-9-0

Moses and the Bible Vol. 3 (1982) ISBN 978-3-9526044-0-3

Moses and the Bible Vol. 4 (1982) ISBN 978-3-9526044-1-0

A series of spiritual lectures channeled through the Soul of Rev. Frank Alper D.D.:

An evening with Christos Vol. 1 (Sept. 1978 – Dec. 1979 ISBN 978-3-9526044-2-7

An evening with Christos Vol 2 (Jan. – Dec. 1980) ISBN 978-3-9526044-3-4

An evening with Christos Vol 3 (Jan. – Dec. 1981 ISBN 978-3-9526044-4-1

An evening with Christos Vol 4 (Jan. – Dec. 1982) ISBN 978-3-9526044-5-8

An evening with Christos Vol 5 (Jan. – Dec. 1983) ISBN 978-3-9526044-6-5

SOUL PLAN by Blue Marsden

RECONNECT WITH YOUR TRUE LIFE PURPOSE

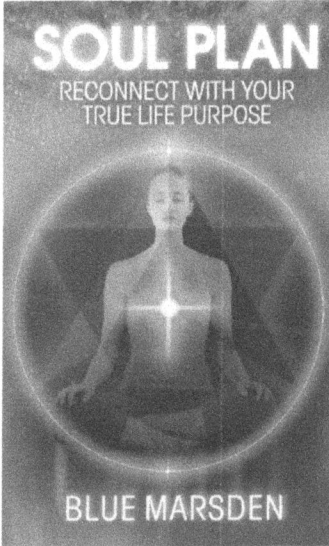

'Soul Plan' is a new interpretation of an ancient system of life purpose analysis. Available now to a wider audience, this method accesses the vibration in your birth name, to determine your entire soul plan.

Moses conveyed the method of Numerology to Dr. Frank Alper, who documented it in Volume 2 of this series. Dr. Alper named this system "The Spiritual Numerology of Moses." Later, he received additional insights and updated the symbols, which are now used by practitioners and students.

In "Soul Plan," Blue Marsden has meticulously compiled and expanded these teachings into a volume that has captivated readers globally and is available in multiple languages. This authoritative guide, enriched with numerous charts and examples, spans 400 pages and is an invaluable resource for anyone seeking a deeper understanding of their soul's journey.

ISBN: 978-1781800768

Length: 400 pages

Embark on a transformative journey today with "Soul Plan" and discover the divine blueprint of your life.